U-Boat War 1914-1918
Volume 2

U-Boat War 1914-1918
Volume 2

Three Accounts of German Submarines
During the Great War

The Journal of Submarine Commander
Von Forstner
Georg-Günther von Forstner

The Voyage of the "Deutschland"
Paul König

The Adventures of the U-202
Baron Spiegel
Von Und Zu Peckelsheim

LEONAUR

U-Boat War 1914-1918
Volume 2
Three Accounts of German Submarines During the Great War
The Journal of Submarine Commander Von Forstner
by Georg-Günther von Forstner
The Voyage of the "Deutschland"
by Paul König
The Adventures of the U-202
By Baron Spiegel Von Und Zu Peckelsheim

First published under the titles

The Journal of Submarine Commander Von Forstner
The Voyage of the "Deutschland"
and
The Adventures of the U-202

Leonaur is an imprint of Oakpast Ltd

Copyright in this form © 2010 Oakpast Ltd

ISBN: 978-0-85706-234-5 (hardcover)
ISBN: 978-0-85706-233-8 (softcover)

http://www.leonaur.com

Publisher's Notes

Contents

PASSENGERS AND CREW LEAVING A SINKING LINER TORPEDOED BY A GERMAN SUBMARINE IN THE MEDITERRANEAN

The Journal of
Submarine Commander Von Forstner

Georg-Günther von Forstner

Contents

Foreword

The following pages form an abridged translation of a book published in 1916 by Freiherrn von Forstner, commander of the first German U-boat. It was written with the somewhat careless haste of a man who took advantage of disconnected moments of leisure, and these moments were evidently subject to abrupt and prolonged interruptions. Many repetitions and trivial incidents have been omitted in this translation; but, in order to express the personality of the Author, the rendering has been as literal as possible, and it shows the strange mixture of sentimentality and ferocity peculiar to the psychology of the Germans.

Part of the book gives a technical description,—not so much of the construction of a submarine as of the nature of its activities,— which presents us an unusual opportunity to glean a few valuable facts from this personal and intimate account of a German U-boat. We are inclined to a certain grim humor in borrowing the candid information given to us Americans so unconsciously by Freiherrn von Forstner, for he could hardly suppose it would fall into the hands of those who would join the fighting ranks of the *hated enemy*, as, in his bitter animosity, he invariably calls the English whenever he refers to them.

Several chapters in this book are simple narratives of the commander's own adventures during the present naval warfare waged against commerce. His attempts at a lighter vein often provoke a smile at the quality of his wit, but he is not lacking in fine and manly virtues. He is a loyal comrade; a good officer concerned for the welfare of his crew. He is even kindly to his captives when he finds they are docile victims. He is also willing to credit his adversary with pluck and courage. He is never sparing of his own person, and shows admirable endurance under pressure of intense work and great responsibility.

He is full of enthusiastic love for his profession, and in describing a storm at sea his rather monotonous style of writing suddenly rises to eloquence. But in his exalted devotion to the Almighty War Lord, and to the Fatherland, he openly reveals his fanatical joy in the nefarious work he has to perform.

It is difficult to realize that this ardent worship of detail, and this marvelous efficiency in the conservation of every resource, are applied to a weapon of destruction which directs its indiscriminate attacks against women and children, hospital transports, and relief ships. Nothing at the present day has aroused such fear as this invisible enemy, nor has anything outraged the civilized world like the tragedies caused by the German submarines.

This small volume may offer new suggestions to those familiar with the science of submarine construction, and it may also shed a little light, even for lay readers, on a subject which for the last three years has taken a pre-eminent place in the history of the War.

Introduction
THE CHALLENGE TO NAVAL SUPREMACY

1

In a letter to William Pitt, of January 6, 1806, relating to his invention of a submersible boat, Robert Fulton wrote prophetically,

> Now, in this business, I will not disguise that I have full confidence in the power which I possess, which is no less than to be the means, should I think proper, of giving to the world a system which must of necessity sweep all military marines from the ocean, by giving the weaker maritime powers advantages over the stronger, which the stronger cannot prevent.

It is interesting to note that, about a hundred years later, Vice-Admiral Fournier of the French Navy stated before a Parliamentary committee of investigation that, if France had possessed a sufficient number of submersibles, and had disposed them strategically about her coasts and the coasts of her possessions, these vessels could have controlled the trade routes of the world. He said also that the fighting value of a sufficient number of submersibles would re-establish the balance of power between England and France.

The history of naval warfare during the last few months has confirmed the opinions of these two authorities, although in a manner which they in no way anticipated.

Direct comparison is the usual method by which the human mind estimates values. We would measure the strength of two men by pitting them against each other in physical encounter; in the same way, we are prone to measure the combative effect of weapons by pitting them in conflict against other weapons. But modern warfare is of so complex a nature that direct comparisons fail, and only a careful analysis of military experience determines the potentiality of a weapon and its influence on warfare. Robert Fulton and Admiral Fournier both indicated that they believed in the submersible's supremacy in actual encounter with capital ships. The war, so far, has shown that, in action between fleets, the submersible has played a negative part. In the Jutland Bank battle, the submersible, handicapped in speed and eyesight, took as active a part, as a Jack Tar humorously put it, "as a turtle might in a cat fight." Not even under the extraordinary conditions of the bombardment in the Dardanelles, when the circumstances were such as lent themselves strikingly to submarine attack, did these vessels score against the fleet in action.[1]

It is easy to understand why the submersible did not take a vital part in any of the major naval actions. In the naval battle of today we have a number of very high-speed armored craft fighting against one another over ranges extending up to 17,000 yards. There is a constant evolution in the position of the ships which it is impossible to follow from the low point of vantage of a periscope, for the different formations of ships mean nothing to the submersible commander. He is so placed that his range of vision is extremely limited, and, on account of the low speed of his boat while submerged, he can operate over only a very limited area of water while the other vessels are moving many miles. Then, too, he is extremely vulnerable to the effect of enemy shells and to the ramming of enemy ships. Under these conditions the submersible commander is more or less forced to a policy of lying ambushed to surprise his enemy. It is said that the *Lusitania* was decoyed into a nest of submersibles. There was but little chance of torpedoing her in any other way. There is also the statement that Admiral Beatty passed with his battle-cruisers through a flotilla of enemy submersibles without being touched.

Submersibles cannot attack their target in definite formations as do surface vessels, and therefore they cannot operate in numbers with the same effectiveness as do the latter. They must maneuver more or less singly, and at random. Being limited to the torpedo, which, when they are submerged, is their sole weapon of attack, they have an uncertain means of striking their armed enemy. The eccentricities of the automobile torpedo are well known; but, even eliminating the fact that this missile is unreliable, the important question of accuracy in the estimate of range and speed which the submersible commander has to make before firing the torpedo must be considered. There is usually a

---

1. The *Majestic* was torpedoed at the Dardanelles, while at anchor. The *Triumph* was torpedoed while moving slowly; both warships had out their torpedo nets.

large percentage of error in his calculations unless the submersible is extremely close to its target. Realizing these limitations, the German submersibles are equipped with small torpedoes, which are generally fired at ranges not exceeding eight hundred to two thousand yards. The necessity of approaching the target so closely is, of course, a tremendous handicap in the general operation of these boats. In view of these facts, it is not surprising that the submersible should not have been able to sweep the capital ship from the seas, as was predicted by certain experts before the war.

2

Admiral Sir Cyprian Bridge regards the functions of defense by a navy as divisible into three main classifications. He says, "The above-mentioned three divisions are called in common speech, coast defense, colonial defense, and defense of commerce." From this classification we are given a hint as to what a sailor means by "naval supremacy," "freedom of the seas," and other terms so misused that today they mean nothing. "Coast defense" means defense against invasion; "colonial defense" means the safeguarding of distant possessions against enemy forces; the "defense of commerce" means such supremacy on the seas as will insure absolute safety of the mercantile marine from enemy commerce-destroyers.

Today every great nation is waging a trade war. The industrial competition of peace is as keen as the competition of war. All the great Powers realized years ago that, to gain and keep their "place in the sun," it was necessary for them to construct navies that would insure to them a certain control of the seas for the protection of their commerce. In this way began the abnormal naval construction in which the Powers have vied with one another for supremacy.

A simple way of looking at the question, what constitutes the power of a fleet, is to consider the warship as merely a floating gun-platform. Even though this floating platform is the most complex piece of mechanism that was ever contrived by man, nevertheless its general function is simple. The war has given us enough experience to convince us that the backbone of a navy is, after all, the heavily armored ship of moderately high speed, carrying a very heavy armament. This floating gun-platform is the structure best fitted to carry large guns into battle, and to withstand the terrific punishment of the enemy's fire.

The battleship is today, notwithstanding the development of other types, queen of the seas. It is therefore not difficult to estimate the relative power of the fleets of different nations. In fact, a purely engineering estimate of this kind can be made, and the respective ranks of the world's naval powers ascertained. Germany has shown all through the war that she thoroughly appreciated the British naval supremacy. Her fleet has ventured little more than sporadic operations from the well-fortified bases behind Heligoland. It was probably the pressure of public opinion, and not the expectation that she would achieve anything of military advantage, that forced her to send her high-sea fleet into conflict with the British squadrons off Jutland.

If one should examine the course of this battle, which has been represented by lines graphically showing the paths of the British and German fleets, one could easily see how the British imposed their will upon the Germans in every turn that these lines make. It reminds one very much of the herding of sheep, for the German fleet was literally herded on May 31, 1916, from 5:36 in the afternoon until 9 o'clock that night. Admiral von Scheer, however, fought the only action which it was possible for him to fight. It was a losing action, and one which he knew, from a purely mathematical consideration, could not be successful.

Through the very definiteness of this understanding of what constitutes naval strength, Great Britain's navy until recently has remained a great potential force, becoming dynamic for only a few hours at Jutland, after which it returned to that mysterious northern base whence it seems to dominate the seas. Because of the potentiality of these hidden warships, thousands of vessels have traversed the ocean, freighted with countless tons of cargoes and millions of men for the Allies. Even at that psychological moment when the first hundred thousand were being transported to France, Germany refrained from a naval attack which might have turned the whole land campaign in her favor.

Today, however, the world is awakening to a new idea of sea-power, to a new conception that will have a far-reaching influence on the future development of naval machinery.

Sir Cyprian Bridge has stated that one of the functions of a fleet is the defense of commerce. There is no more important function for a fleet than this. A nation may be subjugated by direct invasion, or it may be isolated from the world by blockade. If the blockade be sufficiently long, and effectively maintained, it will ruin the nation as effectually as direct invasion.

Thus, in the maintenance of a nation's merchant marine on the high seas, its navy exercises one of its most vital functions. There can, therefore, be no naval supremacy for a nation unless its commerce is assured of immunity from considerable losses through the attack of its enemy. It is idle for us to speak of our naval supremacy over Germany, when our navies are failing in one of their most important functions, and when our commerce is suffering such serious losses. The persons best qualified to judge are those who are most anxious regarding the present losses in mercantile tonnage.

While it has been shown that the submersible of today, as a fighting machine, is considerably limited, and in no sense endangers the existence of the capital ship, nevertheless in the new huge submersible it seems that the ideal commerce-destroyer has been found. This vessel possesses the necessary cruising radius to operate over sufficient distances to control important routes; it makes a surface speed great enough to run down cargo steamers, and has a superstructure to mount guns of considerable power (up to six-inch). It embodies almost all the qualifications of the light surface cruiser, with the additional tremendous advantage of being able to hide by submergence. To be completely successful, it must operate in flotillas of hundreds in waters that are opaque to aerial observation. Germany has but a limited number of these submersibles, otherwise she would be able to crush the Allied commerce.

The ideal submersible commerce-raider should be a vessel of such displacement that she could carry a sufficient number of large guns in her superstructure to enable her to fight off the attack of surface destroyers and the smaller patrol craft.[2] She should be capable of cruising over a large radius at high speed, both on the surface and submerged. The supersubmersible flotillas should comprise fifty or sixty of these units. The attack on the trade routes should be made by a number of flotillas operating at different points at unexpected times. Today Germany has concentrated her submarine war particularly in the constricted waters about England. It is here that the shipping is most congested, and therefore the harvest is richest, but it is also easier to protect the trade routes over these limited areas of water by patrols, nets, etc., than it would be to protect the entire trans-oceanic length of the steamship lanes. If the submersible were capable of dealing directly with the destroyer in gun-fighting, a tremendous revolution would take place in the tactics of "submarine swatting." Then it would be

---

2. The Germans have in operation submersibles of 2000 tons displacement.

17

difficult to see how the submersible could be dealt with.

Improvement in motive machinery is the vital necessity in the development of the submersible. The next few years may see unexpected strides taken in this direction. A great deal will also be accomplished in perfecting methods of receiving sounds under water, particularly in relation to ascertaining the direction of these sounds. When this is done, it will be possible for the submersible commander to tell a great deal about the positions of the vessels above him, and thus his artificial ears will compensate to a great extent for his blindness. By the addition of a greater number of torpedo-tubes, and the improvement of their centralized control in the hand of the commander at the periscope, along lines which we are now developing, it will be possible for the submersible to achieve a greater effectiveness in its torpedo fire. Probably torpedoes will then be used only against the more important enemy units, such as battleships, cruisers, and the like. To be certain of striking these valuable targets would be worth expending a number of torpedoes in salvo fire.

Whether the German U-boat campaign succeeds or not will be largely a question of the number of submersibles that the Central Powers can put into service, and to what extent the submersible will be developed during the present war.

3

German submarines have sunk over 7,250,000 tons of the Allied shipping. In December, 1916, it was stated in the British Parliament that the merchant marine of Great Britain had at that time over 20,000,000 tons. Within the first three months of the unrestricted submarine warfare, 1,100,000 tons of British shipping went to the bottom. At this rate, England would lose 25 *per cent* of her merchant marine *per annum*. It is for this reason that the attention of the entire world is concentrated upon the vital problem of the submarine menace. On land, the Central Powers are still holding their ground, but there is a continuous increase of the forces of the Allies which should lead finally to such a preponderance of power as will overwhelm the forces opposed to them. The Allied armies, however, depend for their sustenance and supplies upon the freedom of the seas. The trade routes of the world constitute the arteries which feed the muscles of these armies. Germany is endeavoring to cut these arteries by the submarine. Should she even appreciably limit the supplies that cross the ocean to the Allies, she will bring about a condition that will make it impossible to augment their armies. In this way there will inevitably be a deadlock, which, from the German standpoint, would be a highly desirable consummation.

Obviously, the first method of handling the submarine problem would be to bottle the German undersea craft in their bases. There has been a number of proposals as to how best to accomplish this. It has been stated that the English Navy has planted mines in channels leading from Zeebrugge and other submarine bases; but it is necessary only to recall the exploits of the E-11 and the E-14 of the British Navy at the Dardanelles, to see that it would not be impossible for the Germans to pass in their U-boats through these mine-fields into the open sea. It will be remembered that the E-11 and the E-14 passed through five or more mine-fields, thence through the Dardanelles into the Sea of Marmora, and even into the Bosphorus under seemingly impossible conditions. Yet, in spite of the tremendous risks that they ran, these boats continued their operations for some time, passing up as far as Constantinople, actually shelling the city, sinking transports, and accomplishing other feats which have been graphically described in the stories of Rudyard Kipling. And again, if the mine-fields were placed in close proximity to their bases, it would be comparatively easy for German submersibles of the Lake type, possessing appliances to enable divers to pass outboard when the vessel is submerged, to go out and cut away the mines and thus render them ineffective.

Nets are also used to hinder the outward passage of the submarine. These nets can likewise be attacked and easily cut by devices with which modern U-boats are equipped. The problem of placing these obstacles is a difficult one, in view of the fact that the ships so engaged are harassed by German destroyers and other enemy craft. Outside of Zeebrugge, shallow water extends to a distance of about five miles from the coast, and it has been suggested that a large number of aircraft, carrying bombs and torpedoes, should be used to patrol systematically the channel leading from that port to deep water, with the intent of attacking the submersibles as they emerge from this base. It is ridiculous to suppose that the Germans would not be able to concentrate an equally large number of aircraft, to be supported also by anti-aircraft guns on the decks of destroyers and by the coast defenses. We have not yet won the supremacy of the air, and it must inevitably be misleading to base any proposition on the assumption that we are masters of that element.

The problem of bottling up the submersibles is enormously difficult, because it necessitates operations in the enemy's territory, where he would possess the superiority of power. I believe that the question of operations against the submarine bases is not a naval but a military one, and one which would be best solved by the advance of the Western left flank of the Allied armies.

The second method is to attack the submarines with every appliance that science can produce. In order to attack the submarine directly with any weapon, it is necessary first to locate it. This is a problem presenting the greatest difficulty, for it is by their elusiveness that the submarines have gained such importance in their war on trade. They attack the more or less helpless merchant ships, and vanish before the armed patrols appear on the scene.

Almost every suitable appliance known to physics has been proposed for the solution of the problem of submarine location and detection. As the submarine is a huge vessel built of metal, it might be supposed that such a contrivance as the Hughes induction balance might be employed to locate it. The Hughes balance is a device which is extremely sensitive to the presence of minute metallic masses in relatively close proximity to certain parts of the apparatus. Unfortunately, on account of the presence of the saline sea-water, the submersible is practically shielded by a conducting medium in which are set up eddy currents. Although the sea-water may lack somewhat in conductivity, it compensates for this by its volume. For this reason, the induction balance has proved a failure.

But another method of detecting the position of a metallic mass is by the use of the magnetometer. This device operates on the principle of magnetic attraction, and in laboratories on stable foundations it is extremely sensitive. But the instability of the ship on which it would be necessary to carry this instrument would render it impossible to obtain a sufficient degree of sensitiveness in the apparatus to give it any value. The fact that the submersible is propelled under water by powerful electric motors begets the idea that the electrical disturbances therein might be detected by highly sensitive detectors of feeble electrical oscillations. The sea-water, in this case, will be found to absorb to a tremendous extent the effects of the electrical disturbance. Moreover, the metallic hull of the submersible forms in itself an almost ideal shield to screen the outgoing effect of these motors.

Considerable and important development has been made in the creation of sensitive sound-receiving devices, to hear the propeller vibrations and the mechanical vibrations that are present in a submersible, both of which are transmitted through the water. There are three principal obstacles to the successful use of such a device: when the submersible is submerged, she employs rotary and not reciprocating prime-movers, being in consequence relatively quiet when running under water, and inaudible at any considerable distance; the noises of the vessel carrying the listening devices are difficult to exclude, as are also the noises of the sea, which are multitudinous; finally, the sound-receiving instruments are not highly directive, hence are not of great assistance in determining the position of the object from which they are receiving sounds[3]

To locate the submersible, aerial observation has been found useful. It is particularly so when the waters are clear enough to observe the vessel when submerged to some depth, but its value is less than might be supposed in the waters about the British Isles and Northern Europe, where there is a great deal of matter in suspension which makes the sea unusually opaque. The submersible, however, when running along the surface with only its periscope showing, is more easily detected by aircraft than by a surface vessel. Behind the periscope, there is a characteristic small wake, which is distinguishable from above, but practically invisible from a low level of observation. Many sea-planes are operating on the other side for the purpose of locating enemy submersibles and reporting their presence to the surface patrol craft. In order to overcome the disadvantages of creating the periscope wake which I have mentioned, it is reported that the Germans have developed special means to allow the U-boats, when raiding, to submerge to a fixed depth without moving.

To maintain anybody in a fluid medium in a static position is a difficult matter, as is shown in the instability of aircraft. One of the great problems of the submersible has been to master the difficulties of its control while maintaining a desired depth. The modern submersible usually forces itself under water, while still in a slightly buoyant condition, by its propellers and by the action of two sets of rudders, or hydroplanes, which are arranged along its superstructure and which tend to force it below the surface when they are given a certain inclination; but should the engines stop, the diving rudders, or hydroplanes, would become ineffective, and, because of the reserve buoyancy in the hull, the vessel would come to the surface.

---

3. Big strides, however, have been made lately in overcoming these shortcomings, and it would appear that the principle of sound-detection is the most hopeful one for us to follow.

In order to maintain the vessel in a state of suspension under water without moving, it would be necessary to hold an extremely delicate balance between the weight of the submarine and that of the water which it displaces. Variations in weights are so important to the submersible that, as fuel is used, water is allowed to enter certain tanks to compensate exactly for the loss of the weight of the fuel. To obtain such an equilibrium, an automatic device controlled by the pressure of the water, which, of course, varies with the depth, is used. This device controls the pumps which fill or empty the ballast-tanks, so as to keep the relation of the submersible to the water which it displaces constant, under which condition the vessel maintains a fixed depth. The principle of this mechanism is, of course, old, and was first embodied in the Whitehead torpedo, which has a device that can be set so as to maintain the depth at which it will run practically constant. With the addition of a telescopic periscope, which can be shortened or extended at will, it will be possible for the U-boat to lie motionless with only the minute surface of the periscope revealing her position.

4

To attack the submersible is a matter of opportunity. It is only when one is caught operating on the surface, or is forced to the surface by becoming entangled in nets, that the patrol has the chance to fire upon it. Against this method of attack, modern submersibles have been improving their defenses. Today, they are shielded with armor of some weight on the superstructure and over part of the hull. They are also equipped with guns up to five inches in diameter, and, affording, as they do, a fairly steady base, they can outmatch in gun-play any of the lighter patrol boats which they may encounter.

One of the important improvements which have been made has resulted in the increased speed with which they now submerge from the condition of surface trim. A submersible of a thousand tons displacement will carry about five hundred tons of water ballast. The problem of submerging is mainly that of being able rapidly to fill the tanks. On account of the necessity of dealing with large quantities of water in the ballast system, the European submersibles are equipped with pumps which can handle eight tons of water per minute.

Again, the speed which the electrical propulsion system gives the vessel on the surface greatly increases the pressure which the diving rudders can exert in forcing the submersible under water. This effect may be so marked that it becomes excessive, and Sueter emphasizes the point that vessels at high speed, when moving under water, may, on account of the momentum attained, submerge to excessive depths. To eliminate this tendency, there is a hydrostatic safety system which automatically causes the discharge of water from the ballast-tank when dangerous pressures are reached, thus bringing the submersible to a higher level where the pressure on the hull will not be so severe. From this it follows that the opportunity of ramming a submersible, or of sinking it by gunfire, is greatly minimized, since the vessel can disappear so rapidly.

A great deal has been attempted with nets. Fixed nets extend across many of the bodies of water around the British Isles. Their positions, doubtless, are now very well known to the Germans. The problem of cutting through them is not a difficult one. Moreover, the hull of the submersible has been modified so that the propellers are almost entirely shielded and incased in such a way that they will not foul the lines of a net. There has also been a steel hawser strung from the bow across the highest point of the vessel to the stern, so that the submersible can underrun a net without entangling the superstructure. Some nets are towed by surface vessels. The process is necessarily slow, and to be effective the surface vessel must know the exact location of the submersible. Towing torpedoes or high explosive charges behind moving vessels has been developed by the Italian Navy, but the chances of hitting a submersible with such devices are not very great.

Bomb-dropping from aeroplanes can be practiced successfully under exceptional conditions only. In view of the fact that such bomb-dropping is exceedingly inaccurate, and that the charges carried are relatively small, this form of attack ordinarily would not be very dangerous for the submersible. Surface craft have also employed large charges of high explosives, which are caused to detonate by hydrostatic pistons upon reaching a certain depth. Patrol boats carry such charges in order to overrun the submersible, drop the charges in its vicinity, and by the pressure of the underwater explosion crush its hull. Since the pressure of an underwater explosion diminishes rapidly as the distance increases from the point of detonation, it would be necessary to place the explosive charge fairly close to the hull of the submersible to be certain of its destruction.

To accomplish this, it would seem that the ideal combination would be the control of an explosive carrier by radio energy directly from an aeroplane. Thus we would have a large explosive charge under water where it can most effectively injure the submersible, controlled

INTERIOR OF A SUBMARINE

by the guidance of an observer in the position best suited to watch the movements of the submerged target.

The third method by which to frustrate the attack of the submersible is to give better protection to the merchant marine itself. While a great deal of ingenuity is being concentrated on the problem of thwarting the submersible, but little common sense has been used. While endeavoring to devise intricate and ingenious mechanisms to sink the submersible, we overlook the simplest safeguards for our merchant vessels. Today, the construction of the average ship is designed to conform to the insurance requirements. This does not mean in any way that the ship is so constructed as to be truly safe. Thousands of vessels that are plying the seas today are equipped with bulkheads that are absolutely useless because they do not extend high enough to prevent the water from running from one part of the ship to another when the ship is partially submerged. Then again, the pumping system is so arranged as to reach the water in the lower part of the hull when the ship is up by the head. Should the ship be injured in the forward part and sink by the head, these pumps would be unable to reach the incoming water before her condition had become desperate.

There is a vessel operating from New York today worth approximately a million dollars, and if she were equipped with suitable pumps, which would cost about a thousand dollars, her safety would be increased about forty per cent. Her owners, however, prefer running the risk of losing her to expending a thousand dollars! If the merchant vessels were made more torpedo-proof, it would be an important discouragement to the U-boat commander. During the past two years of the war, nineteen battleships have been torpedoed, and out of this number only three have been sunk, showing that it is possible by proper construction to improve the hull of a ship to such an extent that it is almost torpedo-proof. While it may not be practicable, on account of the cost, to build merchant vessels along the lines of armed ships, nevertheless much could be done to improve their structural strength and safety; and since speed is an essential factor in circumventing torpedo attack, new cargo-carriers should be constructed to be as fast as is feasible.

So radically have conditions changed that today we have a superabundance of useless dreadnaught power. The smaller guns of some of these vessels, and their gun crews, would be far more useful on the merchant vessels than awaiting the far-off day when the German fleet shall venture forth again. The submersible must be driven below the surface by a superiority of gunfire on the part of the merchant marine and its patrols. In this way the submersible would be dependent upon the torpedo alone, a weapon of distinct limitations. In order to use it effectively, the submersible must be not more than from eight hundred to two thousand yards from its target, and must run submerged at reduced speed, thus greatly lessening its potentiality for destruction. To-day, submersibles are actually running down and destroying merchant vessels by gunfire. If merchant vessels carried two high-speed patrol launches equipped with three-inch guns of the Davis non-recoil type, and these vessels were lowered in the danger zone as a convoy to the ship, such a scheme would greatly lessen the enormous task of the present patrol. In the event of gunfire attack by a submersible, three vessels would be on the alert to answer her fire instead of one: an important factor in discouraging submersibles from surface attack!

The future of the submarine campaign is of vital importance. The prospect is not very cheerful. Laubeuf states that at the beginning of the war Germany had not over thirty-eight submersibles. This statement may be taken with a grain of salt; the Germans do not advertise what they have. It is probable, however, that today they have not more than two hundred submersibles in operation. Over four thousand patrol boats are operating against this relatively small number, and yet sinkings continue at an alarming rate. It is estimated that Germany will be able to produce a thousand submersibles in the coming year and man these vessels with crews from her blockaded ships.

This will be a tremendous addition to the number she has now in operation. The greater the number of submersibles she has in action, the greater the area the submarine campaign will cover. The number of patrol vessels will have to be increased in direct proportion to the area of the submarine zone. Since a large number of patrol boats has to operate against each submersible, it will be seen that a tremendous fleet will have to be placed in commission to offset a thousand submersibles. Thus the problem becomes increasingly difficult, and the protection of the trade route will be no more thoroughly effected than it is today—unless we overwhelm the enemy by a tremendous fleet of destroyers.

1

Ordered to Command a Submarine

Every year about the first of October, at the time of the great army maneuvers, new appointments are also made in the navy; but, unlike our army brothers, who from beginning to end remain permanently either in the artillery, cavalry, or infantry, we officers of the navy are shifted from cruiser to torpedo boat, from the ship of the line to the hated office desk on land at the Admiralty, in order to fit us to serve our Almighty War Lord in every capacity and to the best advantage. The commander of a torpedo boat must be familiar with the service on board a dreadnaught or on any other large ship, for only those who are intimately acquainted with the kind of ship they are going to attack possess sufficient skill to destroy it.

For the first time in the autumn of 190- some of us were surprised at the announcement: "Ordered on board a submarine." This order naturally met with an immediate response, but it brought a new outlook on the possibilities of our career, for we had not yet been trained to this branch of the service which our Almighty War Lord had only recently added to the Imperial Navy. The question was, should we be able to perform this new duty?

It is well known that the French were the first to complete a type of submarine navigable underseas, and the English unwillingly, but with a sly anticipation of coming events, copied this type of boat.

To all outward appearance we kept aloof from following the example of our neighbors, and our chiefs of the Admiralty were beset with expostulations on the subject, but they were silently biding their time while our enemies of today were bragging about their successful experiments with their newly constructed submarines. To the dismay and astonishment of our opponents it was only when the right hour had struck that our navy revealed that it had similar weapons at its command; it therefore prepared for them some disagreeable surprises, and set its special seal from the very beginning on the maritime warfare.

I remember a talk I had with an old army officer a few years ago, when I had just received my appointment to a submarine. We were speaking of U-boats and aeroplanes, and he exclaimed: "Ach! my dear Forstner, give it up! The bottom of the ocean is for fishes, and the sky is for birds."

What would have happened to us in this war had we not so proudly excelled above the earth and beneath the sea?

At first a mystery still veiled our knowledge concerning our submarines; we were told that the dear, good, old U-boat No. 1 had splendidly stood every test, and shortly after, in October, 190-, I went on board, and had the honour later to command her for two years. But during this period, for several years, the greatest secrecy surrounded this new weapon of our navy; strictest orders were given to admit no one on board, not even high officers; only admirals were allowed to penetrate within, and on every matter concerning our U-boats we had to maintain absolute silence. Now, however, that our usefulness has been so fully justified, the veil of discretion can be somewhat lifted, and I can describe within certain limits the life and activities on board a submarine.

2

Breathing and Living Conditions
Under Water

A submarine conceals within its small compass the most concentrated technical disposition known in the art of mechanical construction, especially so in the spaces reserved for the steering gear of the boat and for the manipulation of its weapons.

The life on board becomes such a matter of habit that we can peacefully sleep at great depths under the sea, while the noise is distinctly heard of the propellers of the enemy's ships, hunting for us overhead; for water is an excellent sound conductor, and conveys from a long distance the approach of a steamer. We are often asked, "How can you breathe under water?" The health of our crew is the best proof that this is fully possible. We possessed as fellow passengers a dozen guinea pigs, the gift of a kindly and anxious friend, who had been told these little creatures were very sensitive to the ill effects of a vitiated atmosphere. They flourished in our midst and proved amusing companions.

It is essential before a U-boat submerges to drive out the exhausted air through powerful ventilating machines, and to suck in the purest air obtainable; but often in war time one is obliged to dive with the emanations of cooking, machine oil, and the breath of the crew still permeating the atmosphere, for it is of the utmost importance to the success of a submarine attack that the enemy should not detect our presence; therefore, it is impossible at such short notice to clear the air within the boat. These conditions, however, are bearable, although one must be constantly on the watch to supply in time fresh ventilation.

Notwithstanding certain assertions in the press of alleged discoveries to supply new sources of air, the actual amount remains unchanged from the moment of submersion, and there is no possibility, either through ventilators or any other device so far known in U-boat construction, to draw in fresh air under water; this air, however, can be purified from the carbonic acid gas exhalations by releasing the necessary proportion of oxygen. If the carbonic acid gas increases in excess proportion then it produces well-known symptoms, in a different degree, in different individuals, such as extreme fatigue and violent headaches. Under such conditions the crew would be unable to perform the strenuous maneuver demanded of it, and the carbonic acid must be withdrawn and oxygen admitted.

The ventilation system of the entire submarine is connected with certain chemicals, through which the air circulates, whose property is to absorb and retain the carbonic acid. Preparations of potassium are usually employed for this purpose. Simultaneously, cylinders of oxygen, under fairly high pressure, spray oxygen into the ventilation system, which is released in a measure proportionate to the number of the crew; there is a meter in the distributing section of the oxygen tubes, which is set to act automatically at a certain ratio per man. The ordinary atmosphere is bearable for a long time and this costly method of cleansing the air is used only as a last resort; the moment at which it must be employed is closely calculated to correspond, not only with the atmospheric conditions at the time of submersion, but also to the cubic quantity of air apportioned to each man according to his activities and according to the size of the boat.

It is unnecessary to clear the air artificially during a short submersion, but during prolonged ones it is advisable to begin doing so at an early hour to prevent the carbonic acid gas from gaining a disproportionate percentage, as it becomes then more difficult to control, and it is obvious that it is impossible to dissipate the fumes of cooking, the odors of the machine oil, and the breath of the crew.

Taken altogether one can live comfortably underseas, although there is a certain discomfort from the ever-increasing warmth produced by the working of the electrical machinery, and from the condensation created by the high temperature on the surface of the boat plunged in cold water, which is more noticeable in winter and in colder regions.

It is interesting to observe that the occupations of the crew determine the atmospheric conditions: the quantity of air required by a human body depends entirely on its activity. A man working hard absorbs in an hour eighty-five liters of air. Besides the commander, who is vigorously engaged in the turret,—as will be hereafter described,—the men, employed on the lateral and depth steering, and those handling the torpedo tubes, are doing hard physical work. The inactive men use up a far smaller quantity of air, and it is ascertained that a man asleep requires hourly only fifteen liters of air. A well-drilled crew, off duty, is therefore expected to sleep at once, undisturbed by the noise around them, and their efficiency is all the greater when the time comes to relieve their weary comrades. We had a wireless operator on board whose duties ceased after submersion, and he had so well perfected the art of sleeping that he never cost us more than fifteen liters of air, hourly, underseas.

The length of time that a U-boat can remain under water depends, as we stated above, on the atmospheric conditions at the moment of plunging, and on the amount of oxygen and chemicals taken on board. We can stay submerged for several days, and a longer period will probably never be necessary.

The distance of vision varies somewhat under water, as we look out from the side windows cut into the steel armor of the commander's conning tower. We can naturally see farther in the clear water of the deep ocean than in the turbid, dirty water at the mouth of a river, and the surface of the water-bottom has a direct influence on the sight, which is far more distinct over a light sand than over dark seaweed or black rocks, and at an upper level the sunshine is noticeable many meters under water. But in any case, the vision underseas is of the shortest, and does not extend beyond a few meters; light objects and even the stem and stern of our own boat are invisible from the turret. We are unaware, therefore, of advancing ships, derelicts, or projecting rocks, and no lookout can preserve us from these dangers.

The crew is entirely ignorant of their surroundings. Only the commander in his turret surveys through the periscope now and then a small sector of the horizon; and in turning round the periscope he gradually perceives the entire horizon. But this survey demands great physical exertion, which on a long cruise is most fatiguing. The periscopes erected through the upper cover of the turret must not be too easily turned in their sockets, and the latter are very tightly screwed in, for otherwise they would not be able to resist the water pressure at a great depth. The effort of simply turning the periscope is so exhausting that casual observations of the horizon are made by the officer of the watch; but during naval maneuvers or in time of war, the commander alone manipulates the periscope. It is essential in this case that the periscope should not arise needlessly above water and betray the presence of the U-boat.

The commander must possess the absolute confidence of his crew, for their lives are in his hands. In this small and carefully selected company, each man, from the commanding officer down to the sailor boy and down to the stoker, knows that each one is serving in his own appointed place, and they perform their duties serenely and efficiently.

I have always allowed every man on board once, in turn, to have a look through the periscope; it is their highest ambition, and the result is excellent, for it reassures them and they feel more confident as to their own safety after the granting of this small favor.

As we advance underseas, unless passing through a school of fish, we seldom see any fish, for the noise of the propellers frightens them away; but when we lie at rest on the bottom of the ocean, the electric lights allure them, and they come and stare at us with goggling eyes close to the windows in the turret.

The life, therefore, in our "cylinder" as we call it, offers a good deal of variety. The term "cylinder" is exact, for the inner conformation of a submarine is necessarily rounded, so that relatively thin partitions can successfully resist the greatest pressure of water.

3

Submersion and Torpedo Fire

A new passenger, for the first time in a submarine, has often professed to be unaware that he was fathoms deep under water and has been quite unconscious that the boat had been diving. Of course his astonishment indicates that he was not in the compartment where these maneuvers take place, for it is in the commander's turret that the whole apparatus is centralized for submersion, for steering to the right depth, and also for emersion. At this juncture every man must be at his post, and each one of the thirty members of the crew must feel individually responsible for the safety of the whole in the difficult and rapid maneuver of plunging, for the slightest mistake may endanger the security of the boat.

The central control, situated in the commander's turret, is in reality the brain of the boat. When the alarm signal is heard to change the course from surface navigation to subsurface navigation, several previously designated members of the crew take their post of duty in the commander's turret. The commander, himself, is on duty during the whole of the expedition in time of war, and he seldom gets a chance for rest in his tiny little cabin. Day and night, if there is the slightest suspicion of the approach of the enemy, he watches on the exposed bridge on the top of the turret; for a few seconds' delay in submerging might forfeit the taking of a much coveted prize. So he learns to do without sleep, or to catch a few brief seconds of repose by lying down in his wet clothes, and he is at once ready to respond to the alarm signal of the officer of the watch.

In one bound he is once more surveying the horizon through the periscope, or mounts to the bridge to determine with his powerful field glass whether friend or foe is in sight. His observations must be taken in the space of a few seconds, for the enemy is also constantly on the lookout, and continual practice enables the sailor in the crow's nest to detect the slender stem of a periscope, although the hull of the boat is scarcely visible on the face of the waters.

The commander must come to a prompt decision as soon as he locates the adversary's exact position. Not only may a retarded submersion spoil our plan of attack, but we are exposed to being rammed by a rapidly advancing steamer; our haste must be all the greater if the conditions of visibility are impaired, as is often the case on the high seas, for it takes time for the U-boat to submerge completely, and during this process it is helplessly exposed to the fire of long distance guns.

Calmly, but with great decision, the commander gives the general orders to submerge. The internal combustion engines, the oil motors which, during surface navigation are used to accelerate the speed of the boat, are immediately disconnected, as they consume too much air underseas, and electric motors are now quickly attached and set in motion. They are supplied by a large storage battery, which consumes no air and forms the motive power during subsurface navigation. Of course electricity might be employed above water, but it uses up much current which is far more expensive than oil, and would be wasted too rapidly if not economized with care.

It would be convenient to employ the same oil motor for underseas navigation, but such a machine has not yet been constructed, although various futile attempts of this kind have been made. With only one system of propulsion we should gain much coveted space and a more evenly distributed weight; within the same dimensions new weapons of attack could be inserted, and also effective weapons of defense. The inventor of such a device would earn a large reward. Let him who wants it, try for it!

Quickly, with deft hands, the outboard connections, which served as exhausts for the oil motors, must be closed in such a way as to resist at once the high water pressure. It is well known that for every ten meters under water we oppose the pressure of one atmosphere—one kilogram to the square centimeter—and we must be prepared to dive to far greater depths.

When all these openings have been carefully closed and fastened, then begins the maneuver of submersion. The sea water is admitted into big open tanks. Powerful suction engines, in the central control of the boat, draw out the air from these tanks so as to increase the rapid inrush of the water. The chief engineer notifies the captain as soon as the tanks are sufficiently filled and an even weight is established so as to steer the boat to the proper depth for attack. Notwithstanding the noise of the machinery, large, wide-open speaking tubes facilitate the delivery of orders between the commander's turret and the Central, and now is the moment the commander gives the order to submerge.

All this may sound very simple and yet there are a great many things to consider. In the same manner in which an airplane is carefully balanced before taking wing into the high regions of the sky, a submarine must be accurately weighed and measured before it descends into the watery depths of the ocean. The briny water of the North Sea weighs far more than the less salty water of the Baltic Sea, whose western basin is composed of practically fresh water. A boat floats higher in the heavily salted waters of the North Sea and lies deeper and plunges farther down in the waters of the Baltic. The same U-boat, therefore, must take into its tanks a greater quantity of water ballast in the North Sea, to be properly weighted, than when diving into fresher waters.

Even with small submarines of 400 tons displacement, there is the enormous difference of 10 tons between 1.025 specific weight in the intake of North Sea water and 1.000 specific weight of fresh water. On the other hand, if too much water is admitted into the tanks, the submarine may plunge with great velocity deeper and deeper beyond its appointed depth, and in such a case it might even happen that the hull of the boat could not withstand the overpowering pressure and would be crushed beneath the mass of water. And yet again if too small a quantity of water ballast is admitted into the tanks, the boat may not sink sufficiently below the surface, and thus we could not obtain an invisible attack which is positively necessary for our success.

How much water then must we take in? The answer to this question is a matter of instinct, education, and experience and we must also depend on the cleverly devised apparatus made for this purpose.

The submarine like the airplane must be always maintained at the proper level. The weight of the boat varies continually during a prolonged voyage. Food is devoured and the diving material of the machinery is consumed. The water in which the boat swims continually changes weight and the boat is imperceptibly raised or lowered in a way very difficult to ascertain. The officer responsible for the flooding of the submarine must painstakingly keep its weight under control during the entire navigation. The weight of a meal eaten by each man of the crew, the remains of the food and the boxes in which it was contained, which have been thrown overboard, must be calculated as well as the weight of the water, and the officer employs delicate apparatus for these measurements.

On the open seas these alterations in weight do not occur very rapidly; but whenever a boat approaches the mouth of a river, then the transition from salt to fresh water happens very suddenly and may provoke the undesirable disturbances to which we have already alluded. Also warm and cold currents at different depths produce thermotic conditions, which surprisingly change the weight of the water.

Peculiar as it may appear, a submarine must be lightened to descend to a very great depth, whereas, in steering to a higher level, more water must be admitted into the tanks to prevent our emerging to the surface with too great suddenness. This demands careful attention, skill, and experience.

The principal condition for the success of a submarine attack is to steer to the exact depth required. The periscope must not rise too far above water, for it might easily be observed by the enemy; but if, by clumsy steering, the top of the periscope descends below the waves, then it becomes impossible to take aim to fire the torpedo. The commander therefore must be able to depend on the two men who control the vertical and horizontal rudders, whom another officer constantly directs and supervises.

When the boat has reached the prescribed depth a close examination is made of all the outward-leading pipes, to see if they can properly resist the water pressure; if any tiny leak has been sprung, every cap must be tightly screwed down; for it is evident it would be very undesirable if any leak should occur and increase the heaviness of the submarine. Absolute silence must prevail so that any dripping or greater influx in the tanks can be observed.

Quietly and silently the boat advances against the enemy; the only audible sounds are the purring of the electric motors and the unavoidable noise made by the manipulation of the vertical and horizontal rudders. Alert and speechless, every man on board awaits a sign from the commander, who is watching in the turret; but some time may elapse—now that the periscope is lowered and nearly on the level of the waters—before the adversary becomes visible again. The ship may have changed her course and have taken an opposite direction to the one she was following at the moment we submerged. In that case she would be out of reach and all our preparations prove useless.

At various intervals, the commander presses an electric button and raises and lowers the periscope as quickly as possible, so as to take his own observation without, if possible, being observed himself; for he knows that any injury to the periscope—his most priceless jewel— would, as it were, render the boat blind and rob him of the much coveted laurel leaves. During these short glimpses the commander only perceives a little sky and the wide, round plate of the reflected sea with its dancing waves, while the nervous tension of the expectant crew increases every minute.

At last is heard a joyous outcry from the commander, "The fellows are coming!"—and after one quick glance, to locate the enemy exactly, the periscope is lowered. Now every heart beats with happy anticipation and every nerve quivers with excitement. The captain quickly issues his orders for the course to be steered and for the necessary navigation. The officer in charge of the torpedoes receives the command to clear the loaded torpedo for firing, while the captain quietly calculates, first, the relative position of his boat to the enemy's ship, according to the course she has taken; secondly, at which point he must aim the torpedo to take surest effect, and—in the same way as in hunting a hare—he withholds the shot to correspond to his victim's gait.

Many thoughts fly through his brain. Here, among his companions, the annihilation of the enemy will cause joyful enthusiasm, while among them their downfall will cause overwhelming sorrow. But without doubt they must vanish from the seas, and only a man, who has experienced these sensations, knows how many secondary matters occur to him at such a time.

With lowered periscope, he sees nothing that goes on above him on the sea, and like a blind man the boat feels its way through the green flood. Every possible event becomes a subject of conjecture. Will the fellow continue on the same course? Has he seen our periscope in the second it was exposed, and is he running away from us? Or, on the contrary, having seen us, will he put on full steam and try to run us down with a fatal death stroke from his prow?

At such an instant of high nervous tension, I have caught myself giving superfluous orders to let myself relax, and yet I knew that every man was at his post, fully conscious that his own safety, the safety of the whole boat, and the honour of the Fatherland were all at stake, and dependent on his individual effort. I knew, of course, that each fine fellow, down in the machinery room or at the torpedo tubes, had done his very best, and that all his thoughts were centered like mine in keen expectancy on the firing of our first torpedo—the eel as we call it, guarded with so much love and care—which would speed along accompanied by our warmest wishes. We give nicknames to our torpedoes, mostly feminine names: side by side below lie "the fat Bertha," "the yellow Mary," and "the shining Emma," and these ladies expected to be treated, like all ladies, with the tenderest care and courtesy.

Now comes the announcement from the torpedo officer, "The torpedoes are cleared for firing." He stands with a firm hand awaiting the signal from his commander to permit the torpedo to drive ahead against the hated, but unconscious adversary, and to bore its way with a loud report deep into the great steel flank.

Once again the periscope springs for an instant to the surface and then glides back into the protecting body of the turret. The captain exclaims, "We are at them!" and the news spreads like wildfire through the crew. He gives a last rapid order to straighten the course of the boat. The torpedo officer announces, "Torpedo ready"—and the captain, after one quick glance through the periscope, as it slides back into its sheath, immediately shouts, "Fire!"

Even without the prescribed announcement from the torpedo officer that the torpedo had been set off, everyone knows that it is speeding ahead, and for a few seconds we remain in anxious suspense, until a dull report provokes throughout our boat loud cheers for *Kaiser* and for Empire, and by this report we know that "the fat Bertha" has reached unhindered her destination. Radiant with joy, the commander breathes a sigh of relief, and he does not check the young sailor at the wheel, who seeks to grasp his hand and murmur his fervent congratulations. But congratulations must be postponed until we ascertain that our success is complete.

And once again the periscope runs up towards the laughing daylight, while the commander in happy but earnest tones utters the reassuring words, "The ship is sinking, further torpedoes can be spared." He then permits the gratified torpedo officer, who stands by his side, a quick glance through the periscope to verify the result of his own efficiency. It is chiefly owing to the care of the personnel of the torpedo squad, that the torpedoes are maintained in such perfect condition and that their aim is so correct; and to them is due in great part the success of our attack.

The commander and his officer exchange a knowing look, for they have seen the enemy's ship heavily listing to one side, where the water is rushing into the gaping wound, and soon she must capsize. They see her crew hastily lowering the life boats—their only means of escape—and this is a sufficient proof of our victory. We can depart now in all security. Concealing our presence, we plunge and vanish beneath the waters; having reached a certain distance, we stop to make sure that our victim lies at the bottom of the ocean. We behold the waves playing gently and smoothly as before over the cold, watery grave of the once proud ship and we hasten away from the scene of our triumph.

There is no need of our going to the help of the enemy's crew struggling in the sea, for already their own torpedo boats are hurrying to the succor of their comrades, and for us there is further work to be done.

Imagine the enthusiasm our dear fallen comrade, Weddingen, and his crew must have felt as the loud report of their last torpedo announced the destruction of their third English armed cruiser!

A TORPEDOED SCHOONER

4

Mobilization and the Beginning of
the Commercial War

After long and agitated waiting, we received in the last days of July, 1914, the command to mobilize. Joyful expectation was visible on every face, and the only fear that prevailed was that those of us who were awaiting our orders on land might be too late to take part in the naval battle we were all looking forward to so eagerly.

A few years ago, one of the Lords of the English Admiralty had predicted that in the first naval battle fought between Germany and England, the German fleet would be entirely annihilated. We naturally only smiled in derision at these boastful words. The English newspapers, besides, had for many years announced that whenever German officers met together they drank a toast "To the Day." Although of course this was untrue, yet we were all burning to prove in battle what our great Navy had learned in long, hard-working years of peace.

A mighty engagement at sea seemed to us imminent during these first days of war, and we all longed to be in it. I was, however, at the moment, among those unfortunates who were strapped down to a desk in the Admiralty, and with envy I beheld my comrades rushing to active service, for I had always hoped to lead my old beloved U-boat victoriously against the enemy. We had all placed strong hopes in the part our submarines would eventually play in a great crisis, but we never dreamed that they would so successfully take the first role as our most effective weapon in naval warfare.

With a happiness that can hardly be described, I suddenly received the order to take over the command of a fine, new U-boat which had just been built at Kiel. Never before was a pen more quickly thrown aside and a desk closed than when I handed over my duties in the

German submarines U 13, U 5, U 11, U 3, and U 16 in Kiel Harbor

Admiralty to my successor, and shortly afterwards I took possession of my new, splendid boat, to which I was going to confide all my luck and all I was humanly capable of doing.

I addressed my crew in a short speech, and told them we could best serve our Almighty War Lord in bringing this new weapon of attack, confided to our care, to the highest state of efficiency, and my words were greeted with loud cheers.

There was much work to be done in putting the finishing touches to our submarine, which had only just come off the ways. The auxiliary machines had to be tested and certain inner arrangements made; but, thanks to the untiring zeal of the crew and to the eager help we received from the Imperial Navy Yard, our task was soon accomplished. After a few short trial trips and firing tests, I was able to declare our boat ready for sea and for war, and after everything had been formally surveyed by the inspector we left our home port before the middle of August.

Departing at a high speed, we bade farewell to the big ships still at their moorings, and we soon joined our fellow submarines, who had already in the first fortnight of war, according to an announcement of the Admiralty Staff, made a dash as far as the English coast; and here is the proud record of what they further accomplished: At the beginning of September, 1914, the English cruiser *Pathfinder* was torpedoed by Lieutenant-Captain Hersing, who later sunk the two ships of the line, *Triumph* and *Majestic*, in the Dardanelles and was rewarded with our highest order, *Pour le Mérite*.

This initial success proclaimed our submarines to be our greatest weapon of offense and their importance became of world-wide renown, for we claim the honour of having fired the first successful torpedo shot from a submarine. It opened a new era in maritime warfare and was the answer to many questions, which had puzzled the men of our profession the whole world over. Above all, we had proved that a German U-boat, after a long and difficult voyage, could reach the enemy's coast; and after penetrating their line of defense was able to send one of their ships to the bottom of the sea with one well-aimed torpedo shot. The age of the submarine had truly begun.

Other victories followed in prompt succession. Weddingen's wonderful prowess off the Hoek of Holland, on September 22, 1914, will never be forgotten. In the space of an hour he sunk the three English armored cruisers, *Cressy*, *Hague*, and *Aboukir*, and shortly afterwards dispatched their comrade *Hawke* to keep them company at the bottom of the North Sea.

Let me add to this list the English cruiser *Hermes* near Dover, the *Niger* off the Downs of the English coast; the Russian cruiser *Pallada* in the Baltic; and a great number of other English torpedo boats, torpedo boat destroyers, as well as auxiliary cruisers and transports. All this was achieved before the end of 1914. Unfortunately I am not at liberty, for obvious reasons, to describe my own part in the beginning of the War, but hope to be able to do so after we achieve a victorious peace.

Our dear cousins on the other side of the Channel must have been rather disquieted by the loss of so much shipping at the hands of our boats or of our mines; and they must have realized that a new method of warfare had begun, for their fleet no longer paraded in the North Sea or in any of the waters in the war zone. Their great, valuable ships were withdrawn, and the patrol of their coast was confided only to smaller craft and to the mine-layers, in order that their people might supposedly sleep in peace.

Our adversary was concealed by day, and only ventured forth at night, confident that darkness would insure his safety. This was then the hour for us to lie in watch for our prey, and no more glorious clarion call could have heralded in the New Year than the torpedo shot, which, on the New Year's Eve of 1915, sent the mighty ship of the line *Formidable* to the bottom of the Channel. This was our first triumphant victory, which showed that not even darkness could circumvent our plans, and which dispelled all further doubts as to our efficiency. A few days after the sinking of the *Formidable* a piece of one of the row boats was washed ashore at Zeebrugge, and now adorns our Sea Museum as the only reminder left of the great ship.

We stood at last on the same footing as our dear old sister, the torpedo boat, to whom we in reality owed our present development, and from now on, in proud independence, we were justified in considering ourselves a separate branch of the Navy.

Now that England felt obliged to withhold the activities of her fleet, she instigated against us the commercial blockade and hunger-war; she obliged neutrals to follow a prescribed route; and, by subjecting their vessels to search, she prevented them from selling us any of their wares. In this manner, she sought to redeem herself from the paralysis we had brought on her fleet, and her unscrupulous treatment of the right of nations and her interpretation of the so-called "freedom of the seas" are only too well known.

We retaliated on February 4, 1915, by prescribing a certain danger zone, which extended around Great Britain and Ireland and along the north coast of France. By this interdict, public opinion was enlightened as to the part our U-boats were going to perform in this new commercial warfare, a part, I must admit, that few people had anticipated before the commencement of hostilities. Of course, new demands were to be made upon us; we should have to make long undersea trips, and remain for some time in the enemy's waters, after which we should have to return unperceived. The English called it German bluff, but their tone soon changed after we had made our first raid in the heart of the Irish Channel, and few of them now ventured abroad except when forced by the most imperative obligations.

At the end of October, 1914, the first English steamer *Glitra* was sunk off the Norwegian coast. It carried a cargo of sewing machines, whisky, and steel from Leith. The captain was wise enough to stop at the first signal of the commander of the U-boat, and he thereby saved the lives of his crew, who escaped with their belongings after the steamer was peacefully sunk. If others later had likewise followed his example, innocent passengers and crew would not have been drowned; and after all, people are fond of their own lives; but these English captains were following the orders of their Government to save their ships through flight.

The English authorities even went so far as to inaugurate a sharpshooting system at sea by offering a reward to any captain who rammed or destroyed a German submarine, although the latter could only obey this command at the risk of their lives; but what cared the rulers in England for the existence of men belonging to the lower classes of the Nation? They offered tempting rewards for these exploits in the shape of gold watches, and bribed the captains of the merchant marine with the promise of being raised to the rank of officers in the Reserve. Therefore, the British newspapers were filled with the account of the destruction of German U-boats, and of the generous rewards given for these fine deeds. It was jolly for us on our return to port to read the record of our own doom, and scarcely would there be a submarine afloat if these records had been true.

I should like to tell a short story in connection with these assertions of English prowess. One of their small steamers had actually contrived in misty weather to ram the turret of one of our submarines while it was in the act of submerging. The English captain was loudly praised in all the newspapers and received the promised rewards for having sunk, as he declared, a German U-boat; he had distinctly felt,

he said, the shock of the collision. His statement was certainly accurate, for the submarine was also conscious of the shock, but it was
fortunately followed with no evil results, and our commander had the
joyful surprise, shortly afterwards, when he emerged, to find the blade
of the foe's propeller stuck in the wall of the turret, whose excellent
material had preserved it from serious injury. We happily hope that
the German Empire will never run so short of bronze that it will be
obliged to appropriate, for the melting pot, this fine propeller blade,
which is one of the many interesting trophies preserved in our Submarine Museum.

5

Our Own Part in
the Commercial War and
Our First Captured Steamer

As we have said above, our war against the merchant marine of
the Allied Nations began in February, 1915, throughout the war zone
established around the English and French coasts. Day after day, the
number increased of steamers and sail boats that we had sunk, and
commercial relations between all countries were seriously menaced.
The English were forced to believe in our threats and even the shipping trade of the neutrals had greatly diminished. The mighty British
fleet no longer dared to patrol the seas, and the merchantmen were
told to look out for themselves and were even armed for the purpose.

While the winter lasted, there was not much for us to do, and we
awaited fine weather with lively impatience. During this period, our
victorious armies had occupied Belgium and Serbia, and conquered
the Russian girdle of fortifications. The subsequent participation of
Italy produced but little impression on the fortunate current of events,
whereas Turkey's entrance at our side in the war, opened a new field
of operation for our U-boats in the Mediterranean.

At last, I, myself, was ordered to prepare for a long voyage, which I
welcomed most joyfully after several months of comparative inaction.
We were to remain in the enemy's waters for several weeks, which,
of course, involved the most elaborate preparations. Every portion of
the boat was again minutely inspected, every machine repaired and
thoroughly tested. Like a well-groomed horse we must be in perfect
condition for the coming race. Each man in the crew holds a responsi-

47

ble position and knows that the slightest neglect endangers the welfare of the whole boat. The commander must be certain that everything is completed according to the highest standard. The boat is frequently submerged and performs various exercises underseas, while it is still safe in the friendly waters off our own coast.

We are always abundantly provisioned; for the thirty men must be given the most nourishing food to be fit for their arduous tasks. I have often laughed to see the quantity of provisions placed on deck,—for the dealers, of course, are never allowed to penetrate the inner shrine of the boat,—and yet we have often returned from a long cruise because our food was coming to an end. Every available corner and space is filled with provisions. The cook—a sailor specially trained for the job—must hunt below in every conceivable place for his vegetables and meats. The latter are stored in the coolest quarters, next to the munitions. The sausages are put close to the red grenades, the butter lies beneath one of the sailor's bunks, and the salt and spice have been known to stray into the commander's cabin, below his berth.

When everything is in readiness, the crew is given a short leave on land, to go and take the much coveted hot bath. This is the most important ceremony before and after a cruise, especially when the men return, for when they have remained unwashed for weeks, soaked with machine oil, and saturated with salt spray, their first thought is—a hot bath. At sea, we must be very sparing of our fresh-water supply, and its use for washing must be carefully restricted.

The commander usually spends the eve of his departure in the circle of his comrades, but it is a solemn moment for him as soon as he sails from his native shore. He becomes responsible for every action which is taken, and for many weeks no orders reach him from his superiors. He is unable to ask any one's advice, or to consult with his inferiors, and he stands alone in the solitude of his higher rank. Even the common sailor is conscious of the seriousness of the task ahead and of the adventures which may occur below seas. No loud farewells, no jolly hand, no beckoning girls are there to bid us Godspeed. Quietly and silently do we take our departure. Neither wife nor child, nor our nearest and dearest, know whither we go, if we remain in home waters, or if we go forth to encounter the foe. We can bid no one farewell. It is through the absence of news that they know that we have gone, and no one is aware, except the special high officer in this department of the Admiralty who gives the commander his orders, on what errand we are bound or when we shall return, for the slightest indiscretion might forfeit the success of our mission.

Before dawn, on the day of our departure, the last pieces of equipment and of armament are put on board, and the machinery is once more tested; then, at the appointed hour, the chief engineer informs the commander that everything is ready. A shrill whistle bids the crew cast loose the moorings, and at the sound of the signal bell the boat begins to move. As we glide rapidly out of port, we exchange by mutual signs a few last greetings with our less favored comrades on the decks of the ships we leave behind, who no doubt also long to go forth and meet the enemy.

The land begins to disappear in the distance, and as we gaze at the bobbing buoys that vanish in our wake, we hope that after a successful journey they will again be our guides as we return to our dear German homes. After gliding along smoothly at first, we soon feel the boat tossing among the bigger waves; but we laugh, as they heave and dip around us, for we know everything is shipshape on board, and that they can do us no harm. The wild seas are bearing us onward towards the hated foe, and after all—in the end they lull so peacefully to sleep the sailor in his eternal rest.

In this manner, on a fine March morning, we steered our course to the English coast, to take an active part in the commercial war. Gently the waves splashed around the prow and glided over the lower deck. Our duty was to examine every merchantman we met with the object of destroying those of the enemy. The essential thing was to ascertain the nationality of the ships we stopped. On the following morning, we were given several opportunities to fulfill our task.

It is well known that the English merchantmen were ordered by their Government to fly a neutral flag, so as to avoid being captured by our warships. We all remember how, on one of her earlier trips through the war zone, the gigantic *Lusitania* received a wireless message to conceal the Union Jack and to fly the Stars and Stripes of the United States, but destiny after all overtook her at a later date.

All of us U-boat commanders were told not to trust to the nationality of any flag we saw, and to stop every steamer on our path and to examine her papers thoroughly. Even these might be falsified, and we must therefore judge for ourselves, according to the appearance of the crew and the way in which the ship was built, whether she were in reality a neutral. Of course many neutrals had to suffer from the deceptions practiced by the English, and although their colors were painted on their sides and they were lighted at night by electricity, yet this device could also be copied. Therefore, we were obliged to detain and examine all the ships we encountered, greatly to the inconvenience of the innocent ones.

I will describe the manner in which a warship undertakes the search of a merchantman: Through flag signals the merchantman is bidden to stop immediately; if he does not obey, the warship makes his orders more imperative by firing blank shot as a warning. If then the merchantman tries to escape, the warship is justified in hitting the runaway. On the other hand, if the steamer or sailboat obeys the summons, then the warship puts out a boat with an armed prize crew and an officer to look over the ship's papers. These consist in certificates of nationality, of the sailing port, and port of destination, and they contain a bill of lading as to the nature of the cargo, also the names of the crew and a passenger list if it is a passenger steamer. If the ship is a neutral and her papers are satisfactory, she is allowed to proceed, whereas an enemy's ship is either captured or sunk. If a neutral ship carries contraband of war, this is either confiscated or destroyed, but if it exceeds half the total cargo, then this ship is also condemned.

It is nearly impossible for a submarine to send a prize crew on board a big ship, therefore neutral States have given their captains the order to go in a ship's boat and deliver their papers themselves on board the submarine; but they often annoyed us by a long parley and delay, and it was always with a feeling of disappointment that we were obliged to leave inactive our cannons and torpedoes, the crew sadly exclaiming, "After all, they were only neutrals!"

One sunny afternoon, we were in the act of examining the papers of a Dutch steamer that we had stopped in the neighborhood of the Meuse Lightship, when we perceived on the horizon another steamer coming rapidly towards us, and we judged by its outline that it was of English construction. The steamer we were examining proved to be unobjectionable in every respect, and sailing only between neutral ports, so we dismissed it, and just as it was departing, the English steamer, evidently apprehending our presence, turned about in great haste in hope to escape from us, and steered with full steam ahead towards the English shores, to seek the protection of the ships on the watch patroling the English coast.

The English captain well knew what fate awaited him if he fell into the hands of a wicked German U-boat. Mighty clouds of smoke rose from her funnels, giving evidence of the active endeavors of the stokers in the boiler-room to bring the engines up to their highest speed, and before we had time to give the signal to stop, the steamer was in flight.

Meanwhile we had also put on all steam in pursuit, and drove our engines to their utmost capacity. The English ship was going at a great pace, and we had many knots to cover before we could catch up with her to impose our commands, for she paid no heed to the international flag-signal we had hoisted—"Stop at once or we fire!"—and she was striving her uttermost to reach a zone of safety. Our prow plunged into the surging seas, and showered boat and crew alike with silvery, sparkling foam. The engines were being urged to their greatest power, and the whir of the propeller proved that below, at the motor valves, each man was doing his very best. Anxiously, we measured the distance that still separated us from our prey. Was it diminishing? Or would they get away from us before our guns could take effect? Joyfully we saw the interval lessening between us, and before long our first warning shot, across her bow, raised a high, threatening column of water. But still the Englishman hoped to escape from us, and the thick smoke belching from the funnels showed that the stokers were shoveling more and more coal into the glowing furnace; they well knew what risk they had to run.

Even after two well-aimed shots were discharged from the steel mouths of our cannons, right and left on either side of the fugitive, which must have warned the captain that the next shot would undoubtedly strike the stern, he was still resolved neither to stop nor surrender.

Nothing now remained for us but to use our last means to enforce our will. With a whistling sound, a shell flew from the muzzle of our cannon and a few seconds later fell with a loud crash in a cloud of smoke on the rear deck of the steamer. This produced the desired effect.

Immediately the steamer stopped and informed us by three quick blasts from the steam whistle (the international signal) that the engines would be reversed and the ship stopped. The captain had given up his wild race.

Huge white clouds from the uselessly accumulated steam rose from the funnels, and to our signal, "Abandon the ship at once," the Englishman replied with a heavy heart by hoisting a white and red striped pennon, the preconcerted international sign that our order had been understood and was being obeyed.

This small striped pennon has a deep significance: it means that a captain accepts this most painful necessity knowing that his dear old boat will soon lie at the bottom of the sea; truly a difficult decision for the captain of a proud ship to make. The crew were by this time reconciled to their fate and, as we drew near to parley with the captain, the life boats were launched; the men tossed in their belongings and, jumping in, took their places at the oars. It need hardly be said that we, on the other hand, were pleased with our capture. I have often shaken hands with the gunner who had fired the last deadly shot, for we waste no emotion over our adversary's fate. With every enemy's ship sent to the bottom, one hope of the hated foe is annihilated. We simply pay off our account against their criminal wish to starve all our people, our women, and our children, as they are unable to beat us in open fight with polished steel. Ought we not therefore to rejoice in our justifiable satisfaction?

After the crew had left in two boats the blazing hull of the *Leuwarden* of Harwich, a well-directed shot was aimed at the water line. Mighty jets of water poured into the rear storeroom, and the heavy listing of the ship showed that her last hour had struck. We beckoned to the captain to row up beside us and deliver his papers; he stepped silently on board, and we exchanged salutes. As I saw that the two boat-loads of twenty-five men were lying off within hearing, on either side of us, I took this opportunity to admonish the captain about his foolhardy attempt to escape, and how he thereby had endangered the lives of his crew. The latter, realizing the justice of my remarks, thanked us for having saved them by respectfully lifting their caps. The captain awkwardly excused himself by saying he had simply hoped to get away.

I then notified these people whom we had saved that we would take them in tow to the Meuse Lightship; at this, the fine-looking old captain realized to what useless dangers he had exposed his men, and what cause he had to be grateful to us. With tears in his eyes, he seized my hand and murmured his thanks. I willingly took his outstretched hand. . . . At that instant a Dutch pilot steamboat, which had been attracted to the spot by the sound of firing, hove in sight, and I committed the Englishmen to its care. We all desired, before departing in opposite directions, to witness the final sinking of the steamer, for apparently the English also wanted to see the last of their fine ship, and we awaited the great moment in silence.

We had not long to wait. The stern of the ship sank deeper and deeper, whereas the bow rose sharply in the air, till at last with a loud gurgle the whole steamer was drawn down, and the waters bubbled and roared over the sunken wreck. There was now one less fine ship of the English merchant marine afloat on the ocean!

We had all seen enough, and each one went his way. Our course was pointed westward towards new endeavors, while the Dutchman steered for the nearest port in order to land the shipwrecked crew. I think it was our English friends who waved a friendly farewell from the deck of the pilot steamboat in grateful recognition for our having saved their lives, although they may not actually have wished us "*aufwiedersehn.*"

We read in the Dutch papers a few days later an accurate description of the sinking of the *Leuwarden*, and the English captain was fain to acknowledge how well we had treated him; every captain of an English steamer might have been treated in like manner had not the English Government wished it otherwise.

6

The Capture of Two Prize Steamers

The next day an opportunity offered itself to us which opened to submarines a new field of activity in the commercial war. It was a gray, misty morning, the sea was becalmed, and over the still waters a heavy vapor hung low like a veil before the rising sun. But little could be seen, and we had to keep a sharper lookout than usual to avoid running unawares into a hostile ship, and we also had to be ready for a sudden submersion. We strained all the more an attentive ear to every sound; for it is well known that in a fog, during a calm, we sailors can perceive the most distant noise that comes over the water. In time of peace fog horns and whistles give warning of any approaching vessel, but in time of war, on the contrary, no vessel wishes to betray its presence. It is essential for us to have two men down below, at listening posts, with their ears glued to the sides of the boat, to catch the throbbing of a propeller, or the rush of waves dashing against the prow of a ship, or any suspicious vibrations, for these noises are easily discernible under sea, water being an excellent sound conductor.

On this March morning we were all keenly intent on the approach of some ship; many times already as we stood on the bridge we had been deceived by some unreal vision or some delusive sound; our overstrained nerves transformed our too lively fancy into seeming reality; and in a thick fog objects are strangely magnified and distorted: a floating board may assume the shape of a boat, or a motor launch be taken for a steamer.

I remember a little story about a man-of-war seeking to enter a harbor in a heavy fog; everyone on board was looking in vain for a buoy to indicate the channel when the captain himself called out, "It is for me then to point out the buoy; there it is!" but as they drew near, the buoy floating on the water spread but a pair of wings and flew away in the shape of a gull, and many a gull in a fog may have deceived other experienced seamen.

But to return to our own adventures on this misty morning; we not only saw gulls rising from the sea, and boards floating on the water, but we also encountered English mines adrift, which had parted from their moorings, and to these we thought it safer to give a wide berth. At last the fog lifted, and we discovered in the distance, a few knots away, a steamer; we immediately went in pursuit. Rapidly it steamed ahead, but we caught up with it, and found it belonged to the Dutch-Batavian Line, but as it was steering for the English coast, towards the mouth of the Thames, we took for granted it carried a contraband cargo. We signaled for it to stop, but the steamer refused to obey our command and increased its speed. Having ascertained that we could easily overtake it, we spared our shot, which must be carefully preserved for more useful purposes. After a chase which lasted about three quarters of an hour only a thousand meters remained between us. The Dutch captain wisely gave up a further attempt to escape, and awaited our orders. In compliance with my signal he sent his first officer in a boat with the ship's papers. While we lay alongside the steamer, gently rocking to and fro, the crew and passengers flocked on deck to gaze at us with wondering eyes, and we in return tried to discover to what nationality they belonged.

On reading the papers the officer handed me, I saw the steamer was the *Batavian IV*, destined for London, carrying a cargo of provisions, which is contraband of war. I had to make a rapid decision as to the fate of the steamer, and I resolved to bring the *Batavian* into one of the Belgian ports now in our possession. No U-boat had ever attempted such a feat before, but why not try? Of course we had to cover a long distance with the imminent threat of being overtaken by English warships, but if we did succeed, it was a very fine catch, and after all,—nothing venture, nothing have. Besides the misty weather was in our favor, and it would only take a few hours to reach the protection of our batteries on the Flemish coast.

The Dutch officer was notified that a prize crew would be at once sent on board his steamer to conduct it to the port of Zeebrugge. He opened wondering eyes, but made no protest, for he was fully aware of our cannons turned on his ship and of the loaded pistols of our crew. The crew and passengers on board the Dutchman were no less astounded when our prize command, consisting of one officer and one sailor, climbed up on deck. I could not well dispense, myself, with

The Start: Taking in oil from her tender.

The Chase: Following in the wake of a Dutch steamer.

Overhauling her prey: Rounding the bow of the *Batavier IV.*

The summons to surrender: Calling upon the steamer to heave to

PREY NUMBER TWO: APPROACHING THE *ZAANSTROOM*.

ABOUT TO BOARD THE PRIZE: THE PILOT LEAVING THE TENDER FOR THE STEAMER.

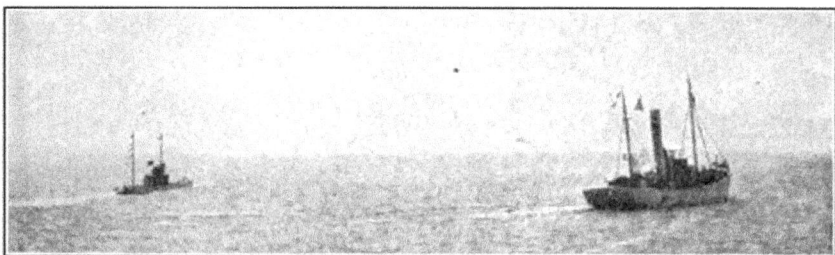

THE TRIUMPH: THE SUBMARINE LEADING THE WAY THROUGH MINE FIELDS INTO ZEEBRUGGE

Von Forstner's Submarine (U 28) In Action in the North Sea
A Series of Photographs taken from the Deck of One of her Victims

more men, and in case my prize was released by the English, it would be better they had so few prisoners of ours to take.

The Dutch captain raised several objections at being led away captive in this manner; above all he was afraid of the German mines strewn before the entrance of Zeebrugge, but my officer reassured him by telling him we should lead the way and he would therefore run no risk. He finally had to resign himself to his fate. So we proceeded towards the shores of Flanders; we, in the proud consciousness of a new achievement, and the Dutchman lamenting over the seizure of his valuable cargo. The passengers must have wondered what was in store for them. Many of the ladies were lightly clad, having been roused in fright from their morning slumbers, and their anxious eyes stared at us, while we merrily looked back at them.

Our officer on board exchanged continual signals with us, and we were soon conscious, with a feeling of envy, as we gazed through our field glasses, that he was getting on very friendly terms with the fair sex on board our prize. We had feared at first that he might have some disagreeable experiences, but his first message spelled, "There are a great many ladies on board," and the second, "We are having a delicious breakfast," and the third, "The captain speaks excellent German," so after this we were quite reassured concerning him.

An hour may have elapsed when a cloud of smoke on the eastern horizon announced the approach of another steamer, and the idea that we might perhaps capture a second prize ship was very alluring. The wisdom of abandoning for a while our first captive was considered somewhat doubtful; if we delayed it might escape after darkness set in, but when I heard my officers exclaim "What a fine steamer!" I decided to try for it. The *Batavian* was ordered to proceed slowly on the same course, and we would catch up with it later; then turning my attention to steamer No. 2, I made quickly in her direction to intercept her on her way to England.

After half an hour's pursuit we signalled for her to stop, and we discovered she was also Dutch. The captain, seeing it was useless to try and escape, put out a boat and came on board with the ship's papers; he seemed thoroughly displeased at the meeting, and hoped no doubt by coming himself to get away more easily, but of this expectation he was to be sadly disabused. On discovering that he was also carrying contraband of war—cases of eggs for London—I ordered him to follow us to Zeebrugge. One officer and a stoker, for I could not spare another sailor, accompanied him as our prize command on board his ship, the *Zaanstroom*, and after a lapse of an hour and a half, followed by No. 2, we caught up with No. 1.

The difficulty of my task can be easily imagined, for I was obliged to make the two steamers follow each other at a given interval and at the same speed; like a shepherd dog herding his flock I had to cruise round my two captives and force them to steer a straight and even course, for one tried occasionally to outdistance the other, probably with the desire to escape in the foggy weather, which increased my fear of not reaching the Flemish coast before dark.

But finally I got the steamers into line, and where persuasion might have failed the menace of my cannons was doubtless my surest reason for success.

My second officer on the *Zaanstroom* signaled that everything was going to his liking and that they were just sitting down to a savory meal of dropped eggs. This was reassuring news, and I could also feel tranquil on his behalf; besides in a few hours we should be safely under cover of our coast artillery. We notified the Pilot Depot by wireless to send us a pilot for each ship, and our messages having been acknowledged we were certain of being warmly welcomed, and that every preparation would be made for the reception of our two prizes.

The closer we got to the coast the heavier the fog lay upon the water, a not unusual experience at sea. We had to advance with the greatest caution; our U-boat led the way to confirm anew the assurance we had given our two steamers that they were in no danger of mines. We had to measure the depth of water repeatedly with the lead, and so doing we had to stop very often; otherwise the lead being dragged by the current draws the line to an inaccurate length. It is but too easy a matter to run aground off the coast of Flanders, as submerged sandbanks are everywhere to be encountered, and this would have been in our present case a most unfortunate occurrence. This continual stopping rather disturbed the order of our march, for steamers are more unwieldy and less accustomed to rapid maneuvering than war vessels. Luckily all went well with us, for after a fine trip of several hours we gladly greeted our German guard-ships lying off the port of Zeebrugge, and the lighthouse on the mole beckoned to us from afar through the thin afternoon mist.

We quickly surrendered our two captive's to the patrol of the port authorities, into whose care and surveillance they were now entrusted. Our job for the day was over, and we could joyfully hurry to our berth within the harbor. We passed along the tremendous stone quay of the artificial port of Zeebrugge; it extends several kilometers, and was built by Leopold II with English money; it had cost many, many millions, and was intended to serve quite another purpose than its present one. We could look with defiance at the mouth of our German cannons that gaped over the highest edge of the jetty towards the sea, as if awaiting the foe.

Farther on up the mole, instead of English troops that the King would so gladly have sent over in transports to march through neutral Belgium and pay us an uninvited visit, stood, side by side, our own brave fellows of the Army and of the Navy. Men from every branch of the service, in their different uniforms, were visible, as they crowded on the pier to witness our arrival with our two prize boats, for the news of this unusual capture had already spread far and wide, and they all wanted to satisfy their curiosity. Their enthusiasm would have been even greater had they guessed that concealed within the hull of our two vessels an Easter feast of undreamed-of dainties lay in store for them. But even without this incentive a tremendous cheer from a thousand throats hailed our appearance as we rounded the mole, and our thirty voices returned as hearty, if not as loud, a three times repeated cheer for the garrison of Zeebrugge. Our tow lines were caught by the eager hands of the sailors, and in a jiffy we were lying securely alongside the quay, safe in port to rest in peace a day or two after a many days' cruise enlivened by such exciting events. Our friends of the Navy, whom we had not seen since the beginning of the war, came to visit us at once; much gay news was exchanged and also sad regrets expressed at the loss of dear fallen comrades.

Shortly afterwards one of the Dutch captains, escorted by two guards, asked me to grant him an interview, and I was glad to make his personal acquaintance; we discussed over a little glass of port wine, which we were both surely entitled to, the incidents of the day, and he gave vent to his affliction at being thus seized, by ejaculating: "A great steamer like mine to be captured by a little beast like yours!" I could sympathize with his feelings, for he had sustained a severe pecuniary loss, and he well knew what would become of his ship and cargo according to prize law, but I suspected he found some consolation in having a companion in misfortune, for the other Dutch captain had to submit to the same conditions. We shook hands and parted excellent friends, knowing that each one of us had only accomplished his duty.

Before making my official report I inspected my two prizes that were docked just behind us; a chain parted them from the rest of the quay, with sentries placed on guard. I gave the preference of my first visit, naturally, as a polite man should, to the steamer with so many of the fair sex on board. I hoped that by appearing surrounded by my officers I should dispel their fear of the "German barbarians." I was told the ladies belonged to a variety troupe that was to give a performance the next evening in London. Poor London, to be deprived by our fault of an enjoyable evening!

Among the other passengers were Belgians and French, who had waited six weeks in Holland for a chance to get across, and also an American reporter of the Hearst newspaper. He had a camera for taking moving pictures, and we discovered later that he had photographed the whole occurrence of the capture of the ship by our submarine. A few days later the *Graphic* of March 27, 1915, published several of his pictures, which eventually found their way to many American papers.

I was ordered that evening to dine with the Commanding Admiral of the Marine Corps, Excellency von Schröder, and a motor called for me and took me to Brügge where he resided. The peaceful landscape and the ploughed fields betrayed but few signs of war, and I saw Belgian peasants and German soldiers planting together the seed for the coming harvest.

While the authorities were passing judgment on my two prizes I had a chance to visit the surrounding country. The English had destroyed in their retreat everything in Zeebrugge, except the new Palace Hotel, the new Post Office, and the Belgian Bank. I made the most of this short opportunity to observe the doings of our men in this conquered land paid for with German blood. I was interested to note how our Marines had been incorporated in every branch of the Army service, and how easily they adapted themselves to this new life. They served as infantry in the trenches, as artillery behind the great coast guns, and also as cavalry mounted on big Flemish mares. They had even been transformed into car conductors on the electric line that runs behind the dunes between Zeebrugge and Ostend. In fact they filled every kind of position, and few Belgians were to be seen. We had created here a second German fatherland and home, notwithstanding the enemy's reports that we had acted like Huns and barbarians, but as neither the country nor the people were of great interest to me my attention was centered on the study of our own troops.

Meantime the unloading of our steamers had begun and I had to supervise it myself. As the cargoes were composed of perishable foodstuffs the usual delays were overcome, and hundreds of sailors and soldiers were ordered to unload the ships. Out of the hold rose newly slaughtered pigs, and sheep, and ducks, which were at once distributed among the various regiments. Two hundred barrels of the best Munich beer were rolled over the quays, and two barrels found their way on board our little boat, which no one could begrudge us. On the *Zaanstroom* there were 4,400 boxes of fresh eggs, each box containing 1,800 eggs, and I was told by an Army officer that every man of the Northern Army received eight eggs for the Easter festival.

On the following afternoon the nationality of the crew and of the passengers was recorded; a number of them were sent as prisoners of war to concentration camps, and many touching farewells ensued between the men and the women who were left behind. The others were taken on a special train under military guard to the Dutch frontier. The German sailors on whom this mission devolved looked very jolly as they sat armed to the teeth in the railway carriages, by twos, watching over two pretty variety actresses, and I think they would willingly have prolonged the journey farther.

I walked along the train to say goodbye to the passengers, who had so unwillingly made our acquaintance, and I was warmly thanked by an old American, to whom I personally had done a small favor, for my courteous treatment; he spoke in the name of all the passengers who had experienced also the greatest civility at the hands of the port authorities. I declined these words of thanks, for they had only received the treatment that was their proper due.

After the train had left, the hour of our own departure had struck; we cast off the lines that had kept us bound for two such memorable days on the Flemish coast. In passing by, I waved a farewell to the two Dutch captains, and away we went—westward ho.

7

Off the Coast of England

Our boat carried us speedily away farther and farther towards the west, and soon the lighthouse on the mole and the outline of the country we had conquered faded away in the evening twilight. Before long we should be surrounded by only hostile shores.

We first sighted the French port of Boulogne where the imposing bronze statue of Napoleon I stands on a marble column fifty-three meters high, with eyes turned towards the English coast. It was built to commemorate the expedition planned by Napoleon in 1803 against the sons of Albion, whose descendants have so recently landed on French soil, and as they lie there encamped, they may wonder, when gazing at the statue of the great Emperor, if he would have welcomed them with the same enthusiasm with which they have been received by the present rulers of France.

On our very first day in the French Channel we were able to sink several steamers, after the crews had left in their lifeboats, and on general lines a similar picture was traced at every sinking. We were now granted our first opportunity to steer a submarine above and below the waters of the North Atlantic. The ocean seemed to rejoice at our coming, and revealed itself to us in all the glory of a March storm. Only those who have seen such a storm can realize its proud majesty. The gigantic, blue-black waves, with their shining crests lashed by the west wind, came rushing onwards into the open mouth of the Channel, and the hemmed-in waters, roaring and surging, dashed themselves against the sharp, rocky points of the French coast, or broke less violently but in ceaseless unrest on the chalk cliffs of England which glimmered white in the rays of the sun.

It is a splendid sight to watch this great spectacle from the high deck of a steamer as it ploughs its way through the foaming flood, or

LIFEBOAT LEAVING THE SINKING P. AND O. LINER ARABIA

to be borne aloft on the top of the waves with a ship under full sail, but it is still more wonderful to behold Nature's great display from the half submerged conning-tower of a U-boat, and to dive through the mountainous breakers until they close gurgling over our heads and hide us from all curious glances. Our little nutshell, in perpetual motion, is drawn down into the deep valleys of the ocean waves, or tossed upwards on the comb of the following breaker. We are soaked to the skin, and the spray covers us like a silvery veil; our boat as well as ourselves is daubed with a salt crust, our eyes smart and our lips have a briny tang, but to us sailors it's a joy to be the sport of the wild waves, and even those few unfortunates who always suffer from sea-sickness never lose their love of the sea.

We were thus, in the midst of a strong southwesterly gale, lying in wait for our prey at the entrance of the English Channel, but no ship was to be seen; most of them took the northerly course beyond the war zone, around the Shetland Islands, and it was not until the next morning, north of the Scilly Isles, in the Bristol Channel, that we caught sight behind us of a big steamer, running before the wind, like ourselves. The wind had somewhat fallen and the March sun was shining bright and warm; the steamer was heading for Cardiff, and we judged by her course that she had sailed from some port in South America.

Turning about and breasting the waves we faced the oncoming steamer and signalled to her to stop; but hardly had she espied us than she also turned about in the hope to escape. She showed no flag to indicate her nationality, so surely we had sighted an English vessel. Even after we had fired a warning shot, she tried by rapid and tortuous curves to return to her former course, and endeavor thereby to reach her home port. Meantime she sent up rockets as signals of distress in quick succession, to draw the attention of British patrol ships that must be hovering in the neighborhood.

This obliged us to fire a decisive shot, and with a loud report our first shell struck the ship close to the captain's bridge. Instead of resigning himself to his fate, the Englishman sent up more signals and hoisted the British flag. This showed us he was game, and the fight began in dead earnest. All honour to the pluck of these English captains!—but how reckless to expose in this manner the lives of their passengers and crew, as we shall see in the present instance.

Circling around us he tried to ram us with his prow, and we natu-rally avoided him by also turning in the same direction. Every time he veered about he offered us his broadside for a shot; with well-directed aim we took advantage of this target, and our successful fire gave him full proof of the skill of our gunners. The latter had a hard time of it; the high seas poured over the low deck, and they continually stood up to their necks in the cold salt water. They were often dragged off the deck by the great receding waves, but as they were tied by strong ropes to the cannons we were able to pull them up again, and fortunately no lives were lost.

On seeing our gunners struggling in the seas, our foe hoped to make good his escape, but with each telling shot our own fighting blood was aroused and the wild chase continued. A well-aimed shell tore off the English flagstaff at the stern, but the Union Jack was quickly hoisted again on the foretop. This was also shot down, and a third time the flag flew from a line of the yard of the foretop, but the flag had been raised too hastily and it hung reversed, with the Union Jack upside down, and in this manner it continued to fly until it sank with the brave ship.

The fight had lasted four hours without our being able to deliver the death stroke. Several fires had started on the steamer, but the crew had been able to keep them under control; big holes gaped open in the ship's side, but there were none as yet below the water line, and the pumps still sufficed to expel the water. It often occurred that in the act of firing the waves choked our cannons, and the shot went hissing through tremendous sheets of water, while we were blinded by a deluge of foam. Of course we were all wet, through and through, but that was of no importance, for we had already been wet for days.

It was now essential for us to put an end to this deadly combat, for English torpedo-boat destroyers were hurrying on to the calls of distress of the steamer. Big clouds of smoke against the sky showed they were coming towards us under full steam. The ship was by this time listing so heavily that it was evident we need waste no more of our ammunition, and besides the appearance of another big steamer on the southern horizon was an enticing inducement to quit the battle scene and seek another victim. We cast a last look on our courageous adversary who was gradually sinking, and I must add it was the first and last prey whose end we did not have the satisfaction to witness. We had been truly impressed by the captain's brave endurance, notwithstanding his lack of wisdom, and we knew that the men-of-war were coming to his rescue. We read in the papers, on our return to a German port, that the *Vosges* had sunk soon after we had departed, and what remained of the passengers and crew were picked up by the English ships. The captain was rewarded for his temerity by being raised to the rank of Reserve officer, and the crew were given sums of money; but all the other officers had perished, as well as several sailors and a few passengers, who had been forced to help the stokers in order to increase the speed of the flying steamer.

We hurried away, therefore, in the direction of the other ship, and as we approached we soon recognized the Spanish colors flying from her flagstaff and painted on her sides. The captain willingly stopped at our bidding and dispatched an officer to us bearing the ship's papers. The stormy waves had somewhat subsided, and although the occupants of the boat got very wet, yet they were able, without danger, to come alongside our submarine. There was no contraband on board the Spanish steamer, and before dismissing the officer I admonished him always to stop at the first signal from a U-boat; he assured me that since the English were constantly hoisting the Spanish flag he had lost all desire to navigate again in the dangerous waters of the war zone. Much relieved at getting away so easily he went on board his own steamer, which resumed its voyage towards the lovely city of Santander on the Spanish coast.

I read an account later of our encounter with the *Agustina* in a number of the *Matin* of April 1, 1915. It was entitled *"Toujours l'U"* and spoke of our undesirable presence in French waters; a following number did us the honour to represent a large picture of our boat with the officers standing on the bridge, taken probably by a passenger on board the Spanish vessel. An arrow pointed to us with the inscription, *"Voila l'équipage de bandits."* The English usually refer to us as "the pirates," and in their rage describe our activities as those of the "German submarine pest." We are accustomed to these flattering allusions, and it amused me to preserve and frame our picture from the *Matin*.

In the next few days we stopped and searched several neutral steamers, and sank many English ones. The captains were occasionally stubborn and refused to obey our signals, so a few accidents occurred; in one case, for instance, a stray shot struck some passengers in a lifeboat, which collapsed; but as a rule passengers and crews were picked up by the many sailboats and fishing boats which circulate in the Irish Sea and in St. George's Channel, and it was we who generally summoned these fishermen to go to the rescue of their shipwrecked countrymen.

The method of capture was always the same, and now, our ammunition being nearly exhausted, we steered a homeward course, with the hope of securing a few more steamers on the way. We were again favored by good luck, for at the entrance of the English Channel we ran across a large steamer, coming from America and heading for a French port, heavily laden with all the fine things that the Americans at present so willingly export.

The chase began in the usual fashion as we followed closely in the enemy's wake. Although the captain made an effort to escape, yet he evidently felt certain from the beginning that he would be unable to do so, for he immediately swung out the lifeboats, ready to be lowered. We were economizing our ammunition and did not, according to our custom, fire a warning shot, but as we drew near the steamer we suddenly saw dark, round objects thrown overboard. The man at the helm beside me exclaimed: "They are throwing mines," but I was not of the same opinion. We proceeded quietly to examine these suspicious objects more closely, and we discovered they were simply bundles of clothes the sailors were trying to save. In pitching them into the lifeboats they had missed the mark and the bundles had fallen into the sea. A report had apparently spread through the English seaports that the men had but scant time to save their belongings when they were sighted by one of our submarines, and since that time their clothes were strapped together ready for a sudden emergency. The steamer stopped and the crew on this occasion took to the boats with a perfect discipline we were little accustomed to witness; the *Flaminian* was sent to the bottom of the sea with one of our last torpedoes.

The following morning, before bidding the west coast of England a temporary farewell, we made another good catch. We sighted a broad-bottomed, four-masted steamer, also coming from America, laden down, as we soon ascertained, with 5,000 tons of oats, and making its way to Havre. We started after it, and as usual it tried to escape, but a well-directed shot through the bridge and chart house brought it to a stop, and it signaled that the engines were being reversed. The boats were lowered, and on drawing near we perceived the captain with others on the bridge holding up their hands as a token of surrender. As soon as those on board had taken their places in the lifeboats they rowed towards us and showed the liveliest interest in the final torpedoing of their steamer. They looked upon it as a new kind of sport, and under the present conditions they could watch the performance in the most comfortable way. The sea was like a mirror, and reflected the smiling spring sunshine whose warming rays were most agreeably felt.

The English captain had scarcely been on board my submarine a moment when he begged that we might go together and verify the excellent aim of our first shot through the forward part of his ship, which he told me had nearly grazed his ear. I consented to go on his lifeboat and admire with him, to our mutual enjoyment, the irreproachable marksmanship of my gunner, although I did not accept a drink of whisky one of the English officers offered me.

On seeing the gaping hole in the forecastle, the captain and his men clapped their hands and cried out, "A very good shot!" The captain congratulated me for securing, as he asserted, the richest prize I had ever made, but I assured him we had sunk even more valuable cargoes than the present one. I decided, as the sea was calm and no ship was in sight, to spare our torpedoes and shells and to put an end to the steamer with little hand grenades. The Englishmen took a sportsmanlike interest in the proceedings, and one of the officers even volunteered to show me the most effective position for the explosive. I naturally did not gratify his wish to place it there himself, for I knew myself very accurately the most vulnerable spot in the ship. In a very few moments a big hole was torn in the side of the *Crown of Castille* and with a gurgling sound the waters rushed in. At the same time long, yellow threads of the finest oats floated far out on the sea and, glistening with a golden shimmer, gave proof long after the steamer had sunk of the precious cargo which had lain within its flanks. You poor French army horses, I fear your rations were cut short for a while!

I had made an interesting study of the manner in which the English crews of the present day were composed. Apart from the British officers there were but few experienced seamen on board. This was made evident by the awkward way the men usually handled the lifeboats. Even with the enormous increase of wages, sailors could not be found to risk their lives in the danger zone, and a lot of untrained fellows, negroes and Chinamen, revealed by their clumsy rowing that they had only recently been pressed into service.

Various other interesting incidents occurred on our return trip, which I shall not mention now, but having safely reached our newly conquered port of Ostend, we read to our amusement in a French paper that our U-boat had been sunk in the Channel by a fleet of six fishing steamers.

We were again warmly welcomed by our comrades from the Army and Navy, all anxious to hear the news we had to tell, and we had the special honour of a visit from H.R.H. the Crown Prince Rupprecht of Bavaria, who, after inspecting our boat, permitted me to give him a detailed account of our recent splendid cruise.

We had many other experiences during the quiet, warm, summer months, with their long, clear nights, which enabled us to achieve the further destruction of a large number of steamers. It was glorious to work in fine weather on our U-boat on the waters of the Atlantic Ocean, so peaceful at this season of the year, and so doing we indulged in much friendly intercourse with the various fishermen we met.

Fishing steamers have replaced the old sailboats to a great extent, and they represent an enormous fishing industry. Our larder was daily replenished with fresh fish, which was a greatly appreciated item on our monotonous bill of fare.

One windy evening in August, we captured a Belgian steamer bringing home coal from Cardiff; the crew having left the ship, the latter was rapidly sinking, when to our astonishment a man sprang on deck from below. He had evidently been forgotten and our shot going through the steamer had warned him of his danger. He hesitated to obey my repeated orders to jump overboard, until finally encased in two life belts he plunged into the water and began to swim; but the screw was still slowly revolving, and he was drawn deep down by the suction of the water. We had given him up as lost, when we were amazed to see him reappear on the other side of the ship. The screw, which had slowly pulled him down, had thrown him up again, and he swam towards us. A big wave having tossed him onto our low deck, we were glad to find he was unhurt, and we gave him the best of care. He was a Dutchman, and after a fortnight spent in our midst, he was so happy he no longer wished to leave us.

When it came to our sinking of the *Midland Queen* a similar incident occurred. A negro had been forgotten by his white fellow-countrymen, and on finding himself abandoned and alone he was so greatly scared that he did not dare to leave the sinking ship; we watched him, and beckoned to him to come to us; but he refused, and swore at us furiously. Presently the *Midland Queen* pitched violently forward, and stood nearly erect with her nose in the water; then with a shrill whistling sound she dived below the surface of the waves. The negro's black head vanished in the turmoil of the waters; then suddenly a loud detonation occurred; an explosion of compressed air within the ship threw up, sky-high, barrels and boards, and among them, to our unbelieving eyes, we saw the wriggling body of the negro. He was projected into the sea, and swam towards us, apparently none the worse after this strange and violent experience. We rescued him and handed him over to his mates, who had rowed back to his assistance.

On our return voyage through the North Sea we met a large sailboat, with the Swedish flag flying from the topmast. She lay completely becalmed, and signaled for us to draw near. We saw a large crowd gathered on her deck, and we approached cautiously, fearing some trap; when to our joyful surprise we found she had 150 German officers and sailors on board. They belonged to one of our auxiliary cruisers, the *Meteor*. Her captain after many exploits had been pursued by several English cruisers, and to save his little vessel from being captured he had deliberately sent her to the bottom of the sea, and the Swedish sailboat had picked up the crew. Our shipwrecked comrades told us they were desperately hungry, but our own provisions were exhausted; so we took them in tow, for not a breath of wind stirred the sails.

By clear sunshine we merrily covered the short distance to our nearest port, and towards midday the sailing ship and ourselves let down our anchors once more off the German coast.

8

The Method of Sinking and Raising Ships

During the present naval warfare we have had the opportunity to watch the sinking of ships of every type and size; shortly after receiving their death wound the vessels usually disappear totally beneath the surface. It takes even big steamers only between four and ten minutes to sink, after being hit by a torpedo or shell beneath the water line, and yet occasionally a ship may float several hours before going down to the bottom of the sea.

It is clearly evident that the slow or rapid sinking of a ship depends on the distribution of its bulkheads and water-tight compartments. A man-of-war, built on the latest models, has a great many small water-tight compartments, for she is meant to be able to continue fighting even after several of these compartments have been destroyed; whereas, an ocean steamer is so constructed that she will remain afloat only a short time after a collision with another ship, or if she runs into an iceberg or a derelict, she can endure a certain intake of water, and lists at a moderate angle far more readily than a warship, whose guns are rendered nearly useless if the ship is heavily canting. A warship must be built so as to withstand, without sinking, the injury caused by a number of gun holes even beneath the water line, where the inner part of the ship must necessarily be subdivided into many parts. A warship is built at great cost, but so is an ocean steamer. The sunken *Lusitania* was worth 35,000,000 *marks* (nearly $9,000,000) and the mammoth steamers of the Hamburg-American Line, the *Imperator*, the *Vaterland*, were still more expensive to build.

The ordinary commercial steamer often has in her inner construction only athwartship bulkheads through the double bottom that run

73

BRITISH HOSPITAL SHIP *GLOUCESTER CASTLE*, SHOWING RED CROSS ON BOW, SUNK IN THE ENGLISH CHANNEL BY A GERMAN SUBMARINE

from one side to another and form large partitions; and in proportion to her height a steamer is again subdivided horizontally into several decks. But these are not usually water-tight, and the cross bulkheads already mentioned form the only water-tight divisions in the hold. In the big cargo spaces, these divisions practically do not exist, and the ship, throughout almost its whole interior, is open from keel to deck. This arrangement, of course, facilitates the rapid loading and unloading of the cargo; therefore, in this type of ship the engine rooms and boilers, surrounded and protected by coal bunkers, are the only really water-tight portions of the ship. Whoever has gazed down into the capacious hold of such a steamer will readily understand that if the water should pour into one of these spaces, at either end of the ship, the other end of the vessel would rise steadily upwards. In nearly every case, even the largest steamer, just before sinking, tilts abruptly its bow or stern straight up out of the sea, until the water rushing into the hold draws the vessel downwards, and with a mighty roar it plunges forever into the deep. We have repeatedly noticed at this moment that the air within the boat escapes with a shrill whistle from every possible aperture, and the sound resembles the shriek of a steam siren. This is a wonderful spectacle to behold!

The velocity with which a ship sinks depends on the size of the hold, and its distance from the ship's center of gravity, for the suction occurs more rapidly if the ship is struck at either end than if the blow is delivered amidships.

We are seldom concerned with ships having empty holds; those we pursue usually carry heavy cargoes, and therefore the water can only penetrate within, where space and air exist; whatever air is left around loosely packed bales and boxes must be driven out before the water can stream in; certain exceptional cargoes, like wool and cereals, absorb a given amount of water, but these can be discounted.

Accordingly the air must escape through existing holes, as the water pouring in drives the air into the hold; the pressure with which the water comes in is equal to the air pressure in the hold. It is quite conceivable that a cargo may be so closely packed that there will be no space left for air to escape, but this is hardly ever the case; frequently, however, the cross-sections of the air vents are so small that the air escapes only very slowly, and the water enters very slowly in the same ratio; under these conditions it would take a long time for a ship to sink. This undoubtedly is very desirable in peace time, but in time of war this is not at all agreeable to our purpose; first, if the foundering of the vessel is prolonged we are prevented from accomplishing other work, and secondly, warships may come to the assistance of a sinking steamer.

Whenever possible we found it expedient to break open with an axe big holes in the lockers in case the hatch could not be quickly enough removed; or, if circumstances did not permit of our doing this, we shot holes with our cannon into the upper part of the steamer, above the hold, so that the air might conveniently escape and the water rush in. We employed, with excellent results, this method in the sinking of many steamers which otherwise would have settled too slowly.

It happens sometimes that a ship may carry a cargo that floats and that is not porous, such as wood. It is impossible to sink a vessel with such a cargo by admitting water into the hold. Shots therefore must be fired at the engine and boiler rooms to force this kind of a steamer to sink. In general this is a safe rule to follow, for these are always the most vulnerable portions of every heavily laden vessel, and this mode of attack is nearly invariably successful.

A warship is usually equipped with cross or lateral bulkheads, in addition to the longitudinal bulkhead that runs from stem to stern through the middle of the ship, dividing it into halves, and other bulkheads separate these two longitudinal sections into further subdivisions. With the exception of the great fast passenger steamers, these divisions by means of longitudinal bulkheads seldom exist on vessels of commerce, although exceptions are to be found.

The sinking of a steamer with a multitude of partitions is effected by its gradually listing more and more on the side in which the water is penetrating, until it capsizes completely and founders with the keel uppermost. A ship can also roll over on its side as it plunges downwards with stem or stern erect.

Theoretically a vessel might sink on a parallel keel, descending horizontally deeper and deeper into the sea; but it never occurs in reality. This hypothesis assumes that a ship has taken in at the bow exactly the same amount of water as at the stern, at exactly the same distance from the center of gravity; this, of course, is impossible; besides the holes through which the water is pouring in must also be at precisely the same level, or else the water pressure would be greater at one end than at the other, and the slightest alteration of level would occasion a greater intake of water and upset the equilibrium of the boat.

There is one other point I will touch upon; it has often been asserted, especially in romances of the ocean, that as a ship sinks the suction creates a tremendous whirlpool which engulfs all things in its vicinity. This statement is naturally very much exaggerated. People swimming about may be drawn down by the suction of the foundering ship, but in my opinion no lifeboat which is well manned is in danger of this whirlpool. Even old sailors, deluded by this superstition, have rowed away in haste from a sinking ship, when they might have stood by and saved many lives.

The question is now often being put, whether it will be possible to raise the vessels that have been sunk during the war. The raising of a ship depends above all upon whether the depth at which it lies is so great that it precludes the work of a diver.

I have already stated that the water pressure augments at the rate of one atmosphere (one kilogram to the square centimeter) to ten meters' increase of depth. If a diver working at ten meters' depth is under a pressure of one atmosphere, at fifty meters he will be under the tremendous pressure of five atmospheres. This is the greatest depth to which a diver can attain, and if by chance a diver has gone a few meters beyond fifty meters, no man to my knowledge has attained sixty meters. The work of divers at a depth of forty or fifty meters is even then not very effective, as they are unable to perform heavy tasks, nor can they remain more than half an hour at a time under such a pressure, and I am speaking now only of experts; therefore only light and easy work can be performed by most divers at a great depth and the appliance of ponderous chains for lifting purposes can only be accomplished under unusually favorable conditions. To raise any ship at a depth above thirty meters must be considered as a very efficient job, whereas if this is attempted at a depth below thirty meters it can be done only by salvage companies where neither unfavorable bottom obstacles nor currents intervene. A strong current renders a diver's work impossible, for it carries him off his feet.

On the high seas the currents change with the ebb and flood. At the precise moment of the turn of the tide the undercurrent is supposed to be nil, and the diver must take advantage of this moment to perform his task. Another difficulty arises from the sand being shifted by the currents, and settling on the prominent parts of a wreck; it often envelops them to such a degree that the ship becomes so deeply embedded in the sand that it is no longer salvable.

According to my estimation eighty *per cent* of our enemy's sunken ships lie from fifty to a hundred meters below the surface of the sea, so that all possibility of their being raised is excluded. The largest ships nowadays have a draft of less than ten meters, and as the vessels sunk lie at far greater depths they are no source of danger to shipping in time of peace. Of the remaining twenty per cent of sunken ships half of them are unreclaimable, either owing to their position, or owing to the high cost of salvage, or because it is not even known where they lie. The other half or last ten *per cent* have probably for the greater part been sunk in channels where the currents are so swift that they are covered with sand, and diving enterprises are out of the question. In time of war such work cannot be thought of; after the war the ships will long since have been completely buried by the sand.

Maybe off the east coast of England one or two ships may be raised, for they lie at a lesser depth and are exposed to slighter currents than on the south coast of England, but in that district only the smaller and more insignificant vessels have been sunk, and it would hardly pay to raise them, especially as they are so damaged by torpedoes and mines that they would probably fall apart on being raised to the surface.

Therefore hardly a single ship will be salvaged, and the sea will retain all those ships it has swallowed in the course of this war carried on by all the nations of the earth.

The Voyage of the "Deutschland"

Paul König

CAPTAIN PAUL KÖNIG, COMMANDER OF THE SUBMARINE
MERCHANTMAN *DEUTSCHLAND*.

Contents

Introduction

The voyage of the submarine merchantman *Deutschland* has, for a long time past, been the subject of eager speculation among the nations of the Old and New worlds.

The wildest rumours regarding the fate of our cruise have appeared in the newspapers, to say nothing of the pretty imaginative stories in which the English have announced again and again that we were stranded or sunk, or, still worse, dispatched to America in bales of cargo.

How often we chuckled on board when our wireless operator picked up one of these nice English wild goose stories from the air!

It is with all the greater pleasure, therefore, that I am now about to start on this account of our fairy-like cruise and adventures. Not that it was such a "fairy-like" business after all. It could hardly be that, for we went as far out of the way of adventure as possible.

Readers must not therefore expect to find in this little book a series of thrilling experiences such as are to be met with in the published narratives of the voyages of battleships. Our task was to bring our valuable cargo to America as smoothly and with as few incidents as possible; to get the better of the English blockade, and to return safely with an equally valuable cargo. This we succeeded in doing, as the following account will show. But as events will prove, things did not by any means always work as smoothly as they might have done, and if at times we were in a pretty tight corner and much occurred that was not on our programme, my readers must thank the amiable activities of the English for all these exciting little incidents.

In spite of such things, however, our enemies were not able to hinder our voyage, though they certainly helped very materially in making it more varied and interesting, and it would be ingratitude on our part not to acknowledge this.

And here I must specially thank my two officers of the watch, Krapohl and Eyring, whose notes have helped to make this account complete. It is impossible for a commander to be always on the conning-tower—I had almost said the "bridge" from force of habit—and six eyes see further than two. For it must be remembered that careful observation is necessary, above everything, on a submarine.

Indeed, a great number of the incidents related here came to my knowledge through the observations of my officers. Throughout the cruise they proved true and unflagging companions, and today they have also become fellow-workers with me in writing this account of the voyage.

My thanks are due to them, even more than to the English, and I trust my readers' gratitude will likewise be extended to them when they have read this book.

The Author

CHAPTER 1

How We Came to Join the "Deutschland" and What I Thought of Her

How did we come to join the *Deutschland*?

That is a long story which I shall leave the authorities to relate. The most important part of it, however, will be found related at the end of this book in the account given of our reception at the Bremen Town Hall after the return of the *Deutschland* from the United States.

To me, the idea of a submarine merchant-man that has been built for long voyages is the tangible expression of the will of the German people to frustrate the effects of the English blockade of the coasts of Germany and America, and of the entire cutting off of our lawful commercial imports.

The Hanseatic enterprise, the technical ingenuity of German ship-building and the workmanlike activities of one of our greatest dock-yards, have united in giving English domination on the sea the biggest blow it has ever had since the Union Jack fluttered over the waves.

At the same time we must not today overlook the changes and developments that are bound to follow in the construction and use of submarine merchantmen. Thus it is possible that the methods of sea warfare will be entirely revolutionised, that new conceptions and conditions of international law will be created, and that changes in the commercial relations of the world will follow which may influence the lives of peoples even more strongly than the present world-war is doing.

We may be proud of the fact that it is a German boat that has ushered in this new epoch.

Our achievement is not to be minimised by the fact that Canadian warships have crossed the Atlantic before us during this war. For they travelled in company, always changing, and accompanied by torpedoboats, cruisers and auxiliaries. They contained only provisions and ammunition, and except for their armament had no dead weight to carry. But their greatest advantage was that they could defend themselves if necessary, whereas the only defence of the submarine merchant-trader lies in submerging. And that is not everywhere possible with a huge, heavy ship of nearly 2000 tons.

Well, I found myself faced with the problem of taking the *Deutschland* to America—an entirely novel and wonderful task. It would have been a new one to me, moreover, if I had not been as I was, an old North German Lloyd captain of a large clumsy steamboat, but a young U-Boat commander.

But to explain this I must first relate how I came across the *Deutschland*. Events moved with surprising rapidity in connection with it. In the middle of October, 1915, I was in Berlin on business. I had then been obliged to leave my bonny steamer *Schleswig* for some time, but the North German Lloyd Company were well acquainted with my whereabouts.

One evening, whilst I was at my hotel, I received a communication, with an urgent invitation to visit Herr Lohmann in Bremen at the Hotel Adlon at the earliest possible moment.

I was surprised. I knew the name of the head of the famous Bremen firm very well, and had been personally acquainted at one time with Herr Lohmann in Sydney, where his firm had been agents for the North German Lloyd Company.

But what did Herr Lohmann want of me, now in these days of war when the "German merchant fleet had been swept from off the seas," as one read daily in the English newspapers? At that time it would have been exceedingly difficult to undertake the management of a German line to the Straits and Australia! And in the Baltic Sea the firm had no trade connections.

What, then, did they want with an old East Asia, America, and Mediterranean captain? Thus I ruminated as I made my way to the Hotel Adlon.

Herr Lohmann received me cordially and did not hold me long in suspense. He alluded to the fine old days in Sydney, asked me how I liked hanging about on dry land, and if I would care again to undertake a long voyage.

What could an old merchant captain say to this, a man who had been practically obliged to leave his ship in an enemy country, and lie about like a wreck on land, while on the other side of the Channel and off the Shetlands the cursed English cruisers lay in wait, and four miles from New York even the American post on neutral ships was overhauled?

I shrugged my shoulders and was silent.

Then it all came out.

Herr Lohmann told me straight away that he was thinking of starting a line of submarine traders to America, and asked me if I would be willing to take command of the first boat. He explained that the first voyage was to be to Newport-News, and asked me, as I had a knowledge through my voyages on the Baltimore line of the North German Lloyd ships, of the waters and depth conditions outside Chesapeake Bay, whether I thought I should be equal to taking such a submarine trader safely across the Atlantic, if the matter really came off.

It was a great plan.

I was never one for weighing pros and cons, and so I said "Yes" straight away. This was indeed a chance for a fellow of over forty-five years, in this war of "black lists" and daily postal robberies, to do something!

"Herr Lohmann," I said, "if the matter really comes off, you can count on me."

And the matter really did "come off."

Barely two months had elapsed when a telegram called me to Bremen for an important discussion. There I saw designs, sketches, and constructional drawings enough to make me open my eyes wide. And when, four months later, during which time I had been by no means idle, I travelled to Kiel, there rose before my eyes on the slips a strange steel object. Trim, comfortable-looking, and quite harmless she lay there, but nevertheless, hidden in its interior, was the realisation of all those detailed, overwhelmingly complicated figures and plans.

I cannot say that the completed reality even then helped to make more intelligible those blue papers with their endless network of strokes and lines, which had so dismayed and bewildered the mind and eye.

Any of my readers who have ever seen in illustrated papers sketches of the control-room or of the conning-tower of a U-Boat will understand this. Indeed, when they are face to face with such a wild medley of rudders, valves, screws, cocks, tubes and pipes, with such a bewildering conglomeration of levers and apparatus, each of which has a highly important meaning and purpose, let them take comfort. My impressions were just the same.

But when this tube-like monster was christened, and her giant grey-green body slipped majestically and silently into the water, she was suddenly transformed into a seafaring vessel, a vessel that swam in her rightful element, as if she had always done so. The first time I trod her narrow deck and climbed into the conning-tower and on to the navigation platform, it was only from her sides, where the green body swelled massively out of the water, that it was possible even faintly to realise how enormous her hull must be.

With proud delight my eyes travelled over the whole structure, as it swayed lightly beneath me, delicacy and strength symbolically blended.

Now I knew that what had hitherto appeared to me as a monstrous product of technical imagination, was a ship, in which I could travel the seas—a real ship—on which an old seaman could set his affections.

Then I laid my hand on the parapet of the conning tower of the *Deutschland* and swore to be true to her.

And in this manner I struck the *Deutschland* and became commander of the first submarine merchant-trader.

CHAPTER 2

The Trial and Departure

And now a strange and wonderful time followed. Day after day, out into the bays, down into the depths. We practised in all weathers and under all conditions.

Every man of the chosen crew realised the task that lay before us. It meant acquiring the art of managing this most delicate and complicated vessel, the last word in bold and skilful construction. It meant learning to know and understand that marvellous wonder-work of modern shipbuilding—a submarine. We had to be in a position to sway, according to our will, this heavy mass of nearly 2000 tons, so that she should obey the least pressure of the rudder, so that she should twist and manoeuvre like a torpedo-boat, so that she should rise and sink in the water like a dirigible in the air.

It meant probing the trustworthiness of the unyielding steel body, the weight and pliability of her mighty machinery; getting on the track of her imperfections or tricks, and coaxing from her the secrets of her mobility and fantastic fish nature.

A submarine is as full of humours as a woman, and as tricky as a racehorse. She is as sober as a tramp-steamer, and as trustworthy as a tug.

She has good qualities and—not good. She can be pliant as a racing yacht and as pig-headed as a mule. And she only obeys him who knows her down to her smallest technicalities.

In this spirit we practised for weeks, round about, above and below water. We studied our boat, and tried not only to become familiar with all her possibilities, but to penetrate into the inner mysteries of this nautical amphibian. And when we returned from the stillness of the bay to the ear-splitting noise of the riveting hammers and the restless hum of the dockyard, we would sit for hours with the constructors and exchange our experiences.

This practical testing gave rise to much stimulating groundwork for new plans and inventions.

It is difficult to express the high esteem I feel for the men of the dockyard at Kiel, or how much I owe to their co-operation. They were untiringly helpful in explaining and testing this wonderful product of their hands and brains, in all its peculiarities. On the very day of our departure the ingenious constructor of the *Deutschland*, Over-Engineer Erbach, came out to our place of anchorage to make a last submerging test.

And at last the day of our departure arrived.

The *Deutschland* was loaded up. The valuable cargo lay well packed in its appointed place, the whole boat was once more overhauled and brought into careful trim.

We laid in provisions for the long journey, and at the last moment even cigars and—gramophone records were brought on board.

With these all our possible wants were securely provided for, and the *Deutschland* was ready for the voyage.

We were ready, too. The farewells from all our dear ones at home lay, God be thanked, behind us; there is always a nasty moment in connection with a cruise into the Unknown, which it is best to get over quickly.

The last to shake us by the hand were the men of the Germania dockyard.

Then the gangway is pulled up, the crew take up their stations, and I climb into the conning-tower.

The steam-tug lies beside us and takes over the hawsers. I call down to the engine-room, "Look out! "and raise my hand. The great moment has arrived.

"Cast off the aft hawsers!"

"They're off."

"Tow away, *Charlotte!*"[1]

The engine telegraph on the stout little steam-tug sounds: the sturdy craft strains at the tow-ropes, and slowly the stern of our *Deutschland* is draw away from her resting-place in the dock.

"Cast off the bow hawsers!"

"They are off."

And with a smack the last hawsers fall from the pier wall into the black, seething waters of the harbour.

1. *Charlotte* is presumably the name of the tug.

Now we are off. I take up the speaking-tube to the control-room:

"Port engines half-speed astern!"

"Starboard engines slowly forward!"

"Rudder twenty starboard!"

"Rudder lies twenty starboard."

Thus the replies from the engine-room come back promptly.

On the conning-tower where I stand next to the helmsman, in front of his little hand-wheel, one hardly feels the movement of the engines.

Only from the churned-up water that seethes foaming and dirty against the rounded body of the *Deutschland*, quickly dispersed to starboard, is it possible to realise that the engines are working.

Slowly the big green whale's back twists and turns, lies first broadside on in the fairway, then slightly to port, then turns with the help of the tug once more to port and astern.

"Stop both engines!"

Slowly the boat moves slightly backwards, pulling at the tow-ropes in its backward movements like some primeval monster. A quick glance from the conning-tower over the trail of water and the pier walls. We have enough room to manoeuvre. The hawsers are cast off, and then both engines are set at half-speed with rudder to port. We turn once more to get well clear of the dock walls where a big grey battle cruiser is being finally equipped. Then I let the rudder lie amidships and order both engines "full steam ahead."

The stern begins to tremble in rhythmical vibration under the increased engine-power, the churned-up water rushes foaming from her sides—the journey begins. Faster and faster the *Deutschland* pushes her way through the dirty waters of the harbour, out into the bay. Our course lies next through the Kaiser Wilhelm Canal to the Wieser, where the shipment of the cargo will be completed. The ship's papers and express post are brought on board by the freighting officials in a special tug, and without any fuss, calmly and secretly the *Deutschland* starts on her remarkable voyage—the first submarine of the world, to whom blockades are unknown—out into the open sea, into the freedom of the ocean.

CHAPTER 3

The First Day at Sea

The North Sea rolls in long swells against us. The weather is clear and the wind blows sharply from N.N.W.

I am standing alone with my first officer on duty on the conning-tower, in the "bath-tub," for thus we have nicknamed the strong shelter which is built round the conning-tower hatch of the *Deutschland*, and which looks like a kind of flying *gondola*. In front of this is the upper steering station, which can, however, only be made use of in fine weather.

Today we stand in oilskins behind the shelter, for the sea is already quite rough enough to wet everything through. The deck is continually swamped, and every minute the waves break over the tower.

I listen with the speaking-tube to the control-room in my hand, while the helmsman growls commands through the telegraph to the engine-room. A dull roar, the bow dips down, foaming, and the waves rush over the deck and dash high against the conning-tower. As quick as lightning we close the hatches and duck in our crackling oilskins behind the shelter . . . this little game is repeated every five minutes.

Between whiles we stand up, listening to the wind rattling in the stays of the masts, and look around us.

For some time the German coast has faded from sight behind us in the S.E., and the accompanying torpedo-boat which travels in front of us is the last bit of the Homeland. Soon we approach the last line of German outposts; four look-out vessels pass by us in single file and signal us "Pleasant voyage."

Our faithful companion now approaches nearer; her crew give us three hearty cheers; the officers on the bridge salute; and we two lonely men on the tower return the salute. Then the little black boat ducks into the sea, makes a beautiful turn, stirring up the foaming water at her keel, grows smaller and smaller, and presently disappears, leaving a thin drifting smoke-flag behind her.

We are left to ourselves, and travel into the Unknown.

Not much time, however, is allowed for thinking. Danger now threatens us from all sides, and I have to make certain that the boat is in good trim, and that I have the engines and submerging appliances well in hand.

I give the command, "Clear everything for a submerging test!"

At once the response comes back from conning-tower and control-room, and the crew hurry to their submerging stations. The oil engines are still throbbing and hammering. Then the alarm bell is sounded and I spring into the conning-tower; the hatches are closed, and at the same time the oil engines cease working.

For a moment one is conscious of a slight pressure in the ears; we are shut up from outside and all is still, but there is no real silence; only a change of sound.

Then comes the command:

"Open the submerging valves!"

"Flood!"

What now follows is so strangely impressive that one could never forget it, once having experienced it. The submerging valves are quickly opened, and with a hiss the compressed air rushes out of the tanks, A gigantic volume of air rises, with such an unearthly snorting and blowing that the pressure in one's ears becomes almost painful. Then the noise becomes more even, and is followed by a loud humming and whistling, and all the high notes of the machinery in the engine-room join together and produce a confusion of sounds.

It is like the strains of some mad, diabolical music that, after the dull, heavy hammering of the oil engines, gives a momentary impression of unearthliness that is at once penetrating and impressive.

This noise in the valves is a sign that the sub-merging mechanism is at work.

The music continues, but in a long downward scale, and during these long drawn out, ever-deepening sounds, one has a bodily feeling as of the rushing in and flooding of mighty masses of water. One seems oneself to grow heavier and to sink with the boat.

Through the window of the conning-tower and by the aid of the periscope it is now possible to observe how the front part of the boat is sinking; the railings are cutting their foaming way through the waves, while the water round the conning-tower rises higher and higher, till everything outside is wrapped in the wonderful twilight of the deep.

Only our faithful lamps are shining. Now it has indeed become silent. The only sound that reaches the ears is the soft swaying rhythm of the electric engines.

Then comes the command:

"Go down to eleven fathoms!"

"Both engines half-steam ahead!"

By the gauge I can follow the depths we are making. Through the flooding we have added several tons of dead weight to the boat. We have made the closed up ship's body heavier than the mass of water displaced—and our giant fish sinks—almost falls—into her element down below.

At the same time we are moving with the electric engines, and the forward thrust of the propeller brings pressure and reaction upon the diving rudder, and transforms the sinking into a downward gliding movement.

When the desired depth is reached, which I can tell at once from the depth gauge, further sinking is prevented by the simple means of making the boat lighter again through pumping out the superfluous water from the submersion tanks.

The furious working of the pumps is thus always the sign that we are approaching the desired depth. Then it stops, only the electric engines continue humming, and from the control-room comes the announcement:

"We are lying at eleven fathoms."

"Boat is trimmed!"

We are travelling at a depth of eleven fathoms. This means that we are practically blind and can only judge our way by the depth gauge and by the help of that carefully protected boat's treasure—the gyro-compass.

No glimmer from outside now reaches us; the periscope has long been swallowed up, and the steel safety shutters in the windows of the conning-tower are tightly closed. We are entirely transformed into the character of a fish.

Now the communications from all compartments, control-room, engine-room, stern-room, bow-room, holds, accumulator rooms, come through without a hitch. We can travel safely with our *Deutsch-land* in the deeps.

It is not always, however, such an easy matter to bring a boat of this size down to a prescribed depth. The changes in the specific weight of the water, owing to varying temperatures or to the different proportions of salt held in solution, play a very important role. How strong an influence this can prove I will show in the difference between the Baltic and North Sea waters.

The specific gravities of the two seas are in the proportions of 1.013 to 1.025. This difference in itself may not appear very considerable. With a boat, however, of the size of the *Deutschland*, for the submersion of which a very heavy excess weight of many tons is necessary, very important consequences are bound to follow from this difference in specific gravity. Thus in order to submerge in the heavier waters of the North Sea it is necessary to make the boat at least seventeen tons heavier than in the Baltic, as otherwise we should not sink.

Moreover, during sudden alterations in the temperature of the water in the bays and river mouths, where the lighter fresh water comes in, the most unpleasant surprises often occur.

Many a U-Boat commander has thought it possible with a certain amount of excess weight to submerge without difficulty and to keep his boat at a fixed depth. Suddenly, however, the pressure gauge registers a greater depth and the boat drops in the water, like an aeroplane which has fallen into an air-pocket, until a test of the specific weight and temperature of the water gives the clue to her behaviour.

It will therefore be seen that such measurements are necessary before the commander can count with certainty on being able suddenly to submerge and as suddenly to reappear above the waters.

In the meantime we have finished our submerging test satisfactorily. All has gone well and each part fully performed its functions. We are in complete control of our complicated apparatus.

Now the command to reappear is given, the diving rudders are set to "up," and immediately I am able by the depth gauge to follow their working and that of our stout pumps.

After assuring myself that there is no noise of propellers to be heard anywhere in our vicinity, and that on all sides there is no likelihood of collision with any steamer, we pass through the dangerous "blind moment."

By this I mean that space of time during which the boat has risen so high that she could be rammed; while, on the other hand, she is still too deep under the water to get the periscope above the surface and take a look round.

This lasts a few minutes. I stand at the periscope and watch. Already the field of vision is lighter. Silvery air bubbles rise up glittering; a blinking and twinkling appears on the glass. Then it is day. A picture arises, clear and shining. The North Sea sways before my eyes with an empty and endless horizon.

Now we are rising to the surface. By the use of the rudder the boat pushes forward faster and faster to the surface of the water. In order to accelerate the ascent compressed air is forced into one of the submersion tanks.

Now she moves very rapidly: the tower is already free. The deck rises dripping out of the water, the conning-tower hatch is opened, fresh air streams in, and I give the command:

"Blow out ballast tanks!"

A wild howling and screeching comes in reply from the control-room, while the powerful turbine engine presses the water out from the submerging tanks.

This does not take long. As soon as a tank is empty the excess air rushes out with a pleasant sound at the side of the boat, and we are soon in normal floating trim again.

We are still using electricity. Now comes last of all the starting up of the heavy Diesel engines by the electric motors.

I have already climbed into the conning-tower and can see nothing of all this, except by the communications from the control-room. Those who are in the engine-room, however, will have an exciting spectacle.

The observation engineers stand at their posts. A command comes through the speaking-tube. Everything is ready. Then the chief engineer gives a shrill whistle, raises his hand, two quick wrenches at the switchboard in the electrical engine-room, a couple of blinding flashes half an inch long: the first valve-heads rise slowly, hesitatingly, as if unwilling, then quicker, a wild report and hissing, a wild irregular spluttering, then the loud explosions become rhythmical, and faster and faster both machines resume their regular vibrations.

The submerging test is completed, and pounding along the *Deutschland* proceeds on her way. The wind does not drop, but the weather keeps fine and the visibility is good.

No steamer comes in sight: we can remain comfortably above water. Nevertheless we need to be extremely careful in our navigation.

So the day draws to its end. But as the sun sinks, dark threatening clouds appear, prophesying bad weather for the following day.

CHAPTER 4

The U–Boat Trap

And thus it turns out. The further we get from land, the rougher grows the sea. The boat is badly tossed about. I notice the roughness of the sea as I lie in my cabin, and towards two o'clock in the morning I am awakened by a "Hullo," from the speaking-tube on the wall at my head.

The watchful second officer, Eyring, announces a white light to starboard which is approaching rapidly.

I spring out, balancing myself round the corner in the control-room, over the ladders, up through the conning-tower hatch, on to the platform.

Eyring shows me at no great distance ahead a white light. It appears to be approaching. We decide not to let it come any nearer, and give the alarm to submerge. Then for the first time I realise the wonderful sense of security that the possibility of such a rapid submersion gives.

It is all quite a matter of course. Here we travel in the middle of this world-war, with an unarmed freight vessel through darkest night. A light approaches. It may be an enemy, it probably is.

In a few minutes a couple of shots may flash out, several shells shatter our conning-tower, the water stream into the ship's body, and in a short while the North Sea close over us.

None of this occurs however. A brief command in the control-room, a few grips of the valves and hand wheels, and we continue our way unhurt, for brutal power may shut us from the surface of the seas, but our enemies in their impotence only cause us to lie a few fathoms deeper. We continue submerged for the sake of safety until daybreak. Towards four o'clock we rise to the surface. It is already broad daylight, but unfortunately also there is a very troubled sea. In the distance we see a couple of fishing-boats laboriously going about their business. We keep them at first sharply under inspection, but quickly discover their harmless character and continue our way over the water.

This process has long ceased to be of a pleasant character. The movements of the boat are such that existence down below in the closed-up compartments, aired only by the ventilator machines, is causing headache and sickness among the men; part of the crew are losing their appetites. Yet it is quite out of the question to remain on deck, which is continuously swept by the seas.

It is somewhat drier on the conning-tower behind the shelter of the "bath-tank" and on the lee side of the tower, which is sheltered from the sea and wind.

Here a few of the watch off duty are huddled together, holding fast to the rails, inhaling the fresh air and shaking themselves when a particularly heavy breaker rolls up round the conning-tower covering them in salt spray.

Thus we travel on the whole day.

A couple of steamers, whose smoke-clouds appear in the distance, we avoid above water by altering our course, after we have made out their route by careful sounding and observation.

This sounds more difficult than it really is. You first of all make sure of the position of your own ship by soundings and calculations, after you have roughly estimated the position of the unknown vessel on the map. If the relative positions of these two are compared on the map with the most important steamer routes, it is possible to judge with some certainty the course the unknown ship must take.

Such a calculation was soon to prove of great importance to us, and was in this case, as will be seen, of great significance.

Towards evening it clears up slightly, and the sea grows calmer. The sun sets under brilliantly illuminated clouds in the west.

All the watch off duty have come on deck to get some fresh air and smoke a hasty cigar or cigarette. Below deck smoking is strictly forbidden. The men are all huddled together on the sheltered side of the conning-tower, tightly packed and pressed against the wall.

It is a strange sight, rather like a swarm of bees, this cluster of men in rough, heavy sea clothes. There is not much etiquette observed here; I know the men have no easy job down below there, and when one of them sticks his head through the tower hatch to draw a few puffs at his pipe, I gladly grant him the short respite.

Moreover, all eyes are fixed unconsciously on the horizon, and this is a good thing. The more men there are to watch, the more can be observed, and many of our crew have the eyes of an eagle.

Suddenly in the clear twilight of the June evening two masts appear in the distance on the port side; a funnel follows, and soon the hull of a steamer appears on the verge of the horizon.

With the help of our excellent prismatic glasses we hold her steadily under observation, our object being to make out her course in order to steer clear of her.

We have soon measured her distance, and I take up the map, compare, reckon, look at the vessel again, then pause bewildered.

From the course she is following the steamer will never reach a port.

Is it possible then?

I call up Krapohl and point out to him my calculations. We have another good look through the glasses, compare maps; they agree.

The fellow is following no route whatever.

In the meanwhile we had approached near enough to make the steamer out distinctly. The twilight of the June evening is so clear and bright that we can observe her with the greatest accuracy. She is a fine steamer of medium size, and carries a neutral flag, while her hull is painted in the colours of her country.

In the middle of the hull is a long double name which we cannot, however, read.

Suddenly Krapohl cries:

"Good heavens! how is it that she is flying her flag so long after sunset? Is it mere chance, I wonder? And what does that extraordinary coat of paint on her hull signify? She is a suspicious looking craft."

I am forced to agree with him.

The apparently aimless course of the steamer fills me with amazement. It is not usual to take a sea-trip on the North Sea for amusement in the middle of this world-war!

We consider what is to be done. As yet the steamer has not sighted us; she continues her mysterious course, and by this time lies a little astern of us.

I decide nevertheless not to submerge, as our courses must soon diverge.

Suddenly the steamer makes a rapid turn and comes straight towards us. Now we can see that the sturdy neutral has swung out her boats; obviously with intent to make more complete her character of a peaceful merchantman, is ready and prepared to follow all commands.

This remarkable civility on her part is quite sufficient for us. I send all the crew below deck and give the alarm at once.

We make ready to submerge, and in doing so move towards the steamer in order to lie broadside on to the sea, which makes diving easier.

Then, to our great amazement, the following incident occurs. Hardly has the "neutral" ship observed our movements and noticed that we are submerging, than she twists round with a jerk.

As we submerge we can still watch her as she wends her characteristic zigzag course, puffing out thick clouds of smoke behind her.

This confession of a bad conscience struck us profoundly. Never have we laughed so heartily as over the flight of this honest merchantman with her unknown course.

The artful dodger thought she was found out, and feared any moment we might send a torpedo into her ribs.

And how furious she must have been! It would have been so fine to approach quite near to the "pest" in the character of neutral ship, and then at a safe distance to let the mask of "harmlessness" drop, and shoot through the port-holes.

The trap was so beautifully laid. The German "pirate" had only to go just a little nearer. Instead we described a curve under water, and only rose to the surface again two hours later.

First I searched the horizon with the aid of the periscope. Then I opened the hatch of the conning-tower, which was still half submerged, in order to get a look round with the glasses. The air was clear. In the south the moon had risen, making the dusky light of the summer night even more transparent. But as far as the eye could see the sea was empty, no steamer was in sight.

The *Deutschland* could continue her way unlighted, and besides our huge delight over the disappointment of the crafty trap-layer, I had now the certainty that we could see all vessels before they could see us. And that was no small matter.

CHAPTER 5

A Somersault in the North Sea

That night, during the darkest hours between eleven and one o'clock, I had decided to travel submerged with the electric engines.

When we submerged in the twilight of the long summer night there had been very little wind, but there was a heavy swell—a sure sign that the wind would rise to a storm within a few hours. Towards two o'clock I gave the order to rise to the surface, and soon noticed from the increasingly wild movements of the boat that the storm had arisen, and that a rougher sea must have set in with it.

At times we made regular springs, but continued steadily blowing out from our tanks and came to the surface in good order.

From the lower end of the periscope I tried to get my bearings. It was, however, almost impossible to see anything, as the periscope was continually enveloped by the heavy breakers, the dim light causing the huge waves to assume monstrous and uncanny proportions.

Now we had risen entirely to the surface, and I climbed into the conning-tower to get a proper outlook over the wildly dancing sea. It had become pleasant weather indeed! In the pale dim light was visible a seething witch's cauldron of tossing, mountainous waves crowned with foam, from which the wind tore away the spray and hurtled it through the air. The boat struggled heavily against it and made little headway. The entire deck was, of course, flooded, and every moment the sea dashed up over the conning-tower and fell over me in showers of spray. I clung on to the parapet of the "bath-tank" and scanned the horizon—a strange outlook, one continually shifting scene of mountainous rollers.

I was just about to give the order to start the oil engines working when—what is that over there?

That dark streak yonder—surely it is a line of smoke? . . .

Then the back of a wave blots it out for a moment from the pale grey sky . . .

I wait, staring through the glass till my eyes ache . . .

There it is again, a dark line of smoke . . . and there, there: a mast-head, thin as a needle, yet I can see it through my glasses; and now . . my eyes are boring their way through the glasses . . . that black thing over there just visible in the valley of the waves . . . the smoke above it, four low funnels . . .

Good heavens! it is a destroyer! . . .

With one bound I spring into the conning-tower, close the hatch: "Alarm!"

"Submerge quickly!". .

"Flood the tanks!"

"Diving rudder; eleven fathoms down."

The commands follow each other in rapid succession. But to carry them out is a different matter!

To submerge head on to this sea will be from all experience sheer madness. . . .

But what am I to do?

The destroyer may have seen us already. . . .

Down we must go, and as quickly as possible.

Below me, in the control-room, the crew are working in speechless haste. The emergency air valves are opened, the compressed air hisses out of the tanks—the submersion valves sing in all their scales. . . .

I stand with compressed lips, looking through the tower window over the tossing sea around me, waiting for the first sign of sinking. . . . But still I can see our deck, still the waves toss us up high into the air. . . . We have no more time to lose.

I order more play to diving rudders, and give the command, "Both engines full speed ahead!"

The whole boat trembles and sways under the increased engine power, and gives a couple of springs; she staggers and reels. Is she never going to sink? . . . Then with a jerk she dips suddenly under by the bow and disappears rapidly at an ever-increasing angle beneath the waves.

The daylight which is just dawning in at the conning-tower window disappears, the depth gauge shows in rapid succession one—one and a half—three—five fathoms. . . . But still the angle of the boat increases.

We stagger, lean backwards, slip over, losing all grip on the floor which is sinking forward . . . I am still just able to hold on to the eye-piece of the periscope . . . and down below in the control-room the men are holding fast on to the hand-wheels of the diving rudders. . .

This lasts for several terrible moments.

We are still wondering what on earth has happened, when suddenly there comes a heavy blow; we are thrown to the ground in all directions, and everything that is not nailed securely down is hurled around us.

We find ourselves in the strangest positions, look at each other, and for a moment a deadly silence prevails. Then the first officer, Krapohl, observes dryly: "Well, we've got there, anyway."

This broke the horrible tension.

We had all grown pretty pale, and now we began to try and face the situation.

What had happened?

Why this unnatural angle of the boat? And why were the engines pounding so madly above us that the whole boat quivered and shook?

Before any of us had time to think, however, our little Klees, the steering engineer, had sprung from his cowering position, and quick as lightning had pulled the telegraph round to "Stop."

As suddenly a deep silence followed.

Slowly we collected our various limbs together and considered: what had happened?

The boat was standing on her head, so to speak, with her fore-part sloping downwards at an angle of thirty-six; her bow must be touching ground while the stern was obediently oscillating in the air above water; the gauge meanwhile showed a depth of about eight fathoms.

I took a rapid stock of our situation; it was far from pleasant.

According to the map there should be here a depth of about seventeen and a half fathoms; judging from the almost upright position of our long boat our stern must be projecting a considerable way above water, making thereby an admirable target for enemy destroyers. As long as the engines continued working it followed that as the waves passed over us the propeller lashing partly in the air was increasing our power of attraction by causing fountains of leaping water and foaming whirlpools.

This Klees had realised through the mad pounding of the engines, and by his presence of mind had removed the greatest danger.

All the same we had marked our resting-place with the strangest of buoys, and expected every moment to hear bombs crashing through the stem of our boat as it hung high in the air above us. . . .

Moments of extreme tension followed. . . .

But all was still. The screws could no longer betray us, and it was probably still too dark above for them to be noticeable. The destroyer, moreover, had no doubt enough to do in looking after herself in this rough sea.

It will be understood, however, that we were particularly anxious to get out of this absurd position as quickly as possible.

As the boat was still quite intact and had sustained the fearful shock without the least damage, the rest of the programme was easy enough to carry out.

The stern tanks which were not quite freed of air were quickly flooded, and so gradually the boat attained a slightly more normal position. Nevertheless, she still lay far from the horizontal. She had stuck her nose too fast in the mud for that!

By this time, however, we were at least entirely under water, and could finish the rest of our work in peace. Part of the water was forced out from the fore ballast tanks, and for the rest we continued trimming the boat with the tanks until the bow became loosened from the ground. Now we began to rise, and were immediately obliged to check her in order to counteract the immediate pendulum-like tendency of the over-weighted stern to descend.

After some time, however, the balance was readjusted and the *Deutschland* was firmly in hand again.

And now we had to consider what could have been the cause of this sudden blunder on the part of our otherwise gallant boat.

A great many circumstances must have combined to produce it. Apart from the fact that it is only possible in rare cases to submerge a heavy boat in a rough sea, it is conceivable that owing to the haste enforced on us by the destroyer the tanks had not been quite pumped out.

The chief reason, however, appeared to be the sudden dynamic working of the diving rudders; this, in combination with full engine power and the downward pressure of a particularly heavy sea, forced the fateful gradient too suddenly. We found ourselves in the position of a dirigible which steers too low before landing, and through a sudden downward current of air is flattened and crushed to the ground by the double weight.

Fortunately for us, the wonderful material of our steel body stood the heavy blow undamaged. Only the bottom of the North Sea may have suffered a little indentation at Latitude X° N. and Longitude Y° E.

One thing more strikes me as worth mentioning in connection with this event.

When I look back in retrospect on my thoughts as we dived at full speed through the deeps at an angle of 36 degrees, I must confess my first thought was for the cargo! Was the cargo safely stored? Could it possibly shoot overboard?

The thought came quite instinctively, strange though it seemed to me afterwards.

I could not shake myself free of the old Adam as captain of a heavy steamer, even on board a U-Boat.

CHAPTER 6

Out Into the Open

We had had more than enough of the North Sea by this time, and were now quite ready to get out into the open.

We were quite clear as to our route, thank goodness. Less so as to what might happen to us on the voyage; but we were prepared by now for any little surprises that might occur. For why travel in a submarine if there are no difficulties to be over-come? After all, many U-Boats had passed successfully through the North Sea and reached the open ocean. Moreover, they had had many dangerous duties to carry out, while we had only to take care not to be seen, and to slip out as quietly as possible.

As a matter of fact, it was not only that we had not to be seen. Our chief care was that we should not be recognised as a U-Boat trader.

The peculiar character of the *Deutschland* as a peaceful unarmed merchant trader would not have protected us in the least from being sunk at sight. Of that we were convinced, and how right we were was seen in the later English and French official declarations.

If we were once recognised as a U-Boat trader, we should have been not only in danger every minute, but our unhampered arrival at the American port of our destination would be highly endangered. We should have had a whole pack of thirsty blood-hounds in our wake. We hoped therefore to take the whole world by surprise by our arrival in America, and all our ambitions were strained towards this achievement.

Thus I meditated as we neared the danger zone.

We moved forward therefore with great caution. We saw a great deal in the process, were seen ourselves extremely seldom; recognised never. During the day we avoided several steamers by altering our course. At night we travelled with darkened lights, submerging when necessary.

The weather also favoured us. Once we sighted an English auxiliary cruiser some distance off; she was travelling in a definite direction with a zigzag course. For some time we held a parallel course with her, keeping her carefully under observation. But owing to the high seas, which must have made her navigation far from pleasant, we remained unnoticed.

On another occasion a lookout vessel approached us in the evening twilight; she had seen us and hailed us with the English merchant flag to signify harmlessness and thus mislead us for an attack.

As we continued calmly on our way she moved off in vexation. The sea was probably too rough for her to seek further communication with us.

We were easily able to avoid other look-out vessels, travelling at an even higher rate.

Later on it grew calm—and misty. We submerged and came to rest on the bottom. We were in no hurry, and why should we not take a little rest?

It was not what might be called exactly shallow in that spot; it was, in fact, extremely deep. All the more calm and safe a resting-place. For what else were our excellent deep-sea lead machine, and the wonderfully stout body of our *Deutschland*?

That night on the bed of the ocean at X—— was a great relaxation for us all. We were able once more to have a good wash and rest without fear of being immediately awakened by a "Hullo "from the speaking-tube.

But first of all we dined—a real, proper dinner. The two gramophones played gaily, and we clinked our glasses together, which were filled—possibly out of compliment—with French champagne.

Our faithful Stucke—steward, second cook, and servant to us all—waited on us with earnest solemnity, just as if he were still steward in the dining-room of the *Kronprinzessin Cëcilie*. It was impossible to imagine that he had been a prisoner in France for nearly a year. It was as if he had always haunted the *Deutschland* at a depth of ten fathoms below the sea, where in our comfortable mess-room he was continually developing fresh arts and contrivances, and had stored away in the miniature pantry and a couple of drawers an undreamed-of amount of table linen and plate.

Next morning we go up to the surface again. The pump rattles and growls and we climb with several hundred gallons over normal weight, and with the diving rudders in perfect working order, to the surface.

At about eleven fathoms the boat begins to lose her beautiful steadiness. This is first noticeable on the gauge, afterwards by the diving rudders which are harder to manipulate and on which the boat often presses heavily. The higher we rise the more powerful these movements become, so there must be a pretty rough sea up above.

We rise now carefully up to periscope depth, travel thus for a while and look around. Except for a wide sweep of foaming waves nothing is to be seen. The weather suits me exactly, for we can diminish our watchfulness accordingly.

I now decide to rise entirely to the surface, and fill one of the tanks with compressed air till the conning-tower is sufficiently free. The oil engines are started, and the ventilation machine makes ready to take in a fresh supply of air. Hardly have we opened the hatch of the conning-tower, however, when a rough, watery greeting flies down into the control-room. We are not quite ready apparently. Another tank is blown out and the turbo-fan set in motion till the tanks are soon quite empty.

But first another little trick of seamanship has to be brought into play.

In order to rise still higher we have to get her broadside on again, for in this wild sea the long, heavy body of the boat will not rise easily out of the water head on.

Moving slowly we turn the *Deutschland* broadside on to the sea. She rolls horribly, nearly shaking the soul out of your body. Added to this, the heavy cross-seas are sweeping continuously over the boat. But she obeys the diving rudders and slowly raises her nose out of the water. As we rise entirely to the surface the conning-tower and periscope sway alarmingly in the air.

Now comes another unpleasant moment. It is necessary to bring the boat at slow speed again on to her proper course.

Sheltering behind the thick windows of the conning-tower, on which the spray streams down incessantly, with arms and legs wedged firmly against the sides, I peer around.

From old experience of the sea, I am waiting for three particularly heavy waves to pass over, which are usually followed by a low irregular one. Now the third big wave has passed. There is a call to the helmsman in the control-room; it works. The bow bores her way slowly round, and we are back on our old course again without meeting any particularly heavy breakers.

It is still a pretty tough job all the same. The storm, if anything, increases, and our journey proceeds but slowly against the heavy sea. Added to this, part of the crew are seasick; and the short, backward pitches of the boat are horrible. But as we proceed, the long steady swell of the Atlantic Ocean becomes more marked. The short, pitching movements gradually cease and change into a majestic swaying.

In the distance we see two English cruisers returning from their nightly reconnoitre. We lie too low for them to notice us, and they disappear rapidly in the opposite direction.

Now we are free from the English outpost boats, and steer cheerfully out into the wide open spaces of the Atlantic.

CHAPTER 7

In the Atlantic

At last we were out in the open.

The Atlantic did not receive us in a very friendly manner it must be confessed.

We had grown used to a good deal in the last few days, but I was anxious to spare the nerves of the crew as much as possible, on account of the long journey that lay before us. I decided therefore to take a more southerly direction, in order to try and hit on fairer weather if possible. Unfortunately we were to be disappointed in this, as will be seen.

As I glance today through my notes of those first days in the Atlantic, I continually come across remarks of this kind: "Heavy Sea," "Stiff wind from the W.N.W., Strength 8," "Wind blowing up for a storm," "Heavy seas rolling over the whole boat and even over the conning-tower," "Boat travelling almost continuously under water," etc. In these few curt sentences lies the history of the hard and nerve-racking existence of twenty-nine men, shut up in the body of a steel fish, as she made her way untiringly through the wild tossing seas.

I know of no better opportunity of praising the excellently thought-out construction and the perfect seafaring qualities of our *Deutschland* than in calling to mind those stormy days in the Atlantic. The elements certainly did not help to make our journey to America an easy one. The highest possible demands were made on the body and machinery of the boat, which had to be continually at work day after day in order that we might reach our destination.

And here I cannot help thinking with gratitude of the dockyard and all the men whose work had contributed to help us complete our journey by giving this wonderful piece of sea-craft mechanism into our hands.

It is easy to wax enthusiastic over a fine ship, that delights the eye of every onlooker when in harbour by her elegance, and extracts the admiration of the expert and the uninitiated by her rapid movement in smooth waters. But the real inner worth of a ship is only to be discovered when she has completed her test on the high seas. Then, and only then, you learn her best qualities and gain that real confidence in her trustworthiness and sea-faring capabilities, when the wind is blowing with a strength 10, and the sea has a roughness 8, during which you must go head on. And this not only for a couple of hours, but day after day, week after week. Only then can a ship prove what she is really worth.

This is particularly the case with a U-Boat in war time. A merchantman in peace time has very often a severe strain in holding out, but she has always the possibility of seeking a port of refuge, or of hailing assistance. At the worst, she can drift a few days and wait for smoother weather. None of this is possible with the U-Boat. To the dangers of the sea are added the dangers from the enemy, the cruellest and most pitiless of enemies. No haven of refuge beckons to her, and if she were to lie for a few minutes helpless and be discovered, her adversaries, who would have helped a damaged steamer in distress, would loosen the greedy blood-hounds at her throat.

No one is so lonely and entirely dependent on himself as a U-Boat captain. If he cannot absolutely rely on his vessel, then he is lost.

It is for this reason that we realised how much we owed to the Germania docks and to the chief engineer, Erbach, the inventor of our boat. It was his plans combined with the splendid co-operation of the submarine builders and shipping officials that had given birth to this wonderful seafaring vessel. The boat which in the winter of 1915 arose on the slips at Kiel, in so short a space of time and yet with the precision of accurate workmanship, and which Herr Erbach taught me to work and understand on that memorable test voyage early in the year, was now two months later bravely ploughing her way through the stormy seas, carrying the fame of German shipbuilding across the ocean.

★★★★★★★

The *Deutschland* had therefore been severely tested, and had come through with flying colours. For several days the weather remained the same, with hurricane gusts lathing up the water into crashing mountains of waves.

111

All the deck hatches were, of necessity, closed, and at times even the conning-tower hatch, which was so well sheltered by the "bath-tank," had to be closed by the watch-officer at every onrush of the waves.

It was far from pleasant in the conning-tower. But below deck, where the men were suffering badly from sea-sickness in the close atmosphere and with the incessant rolling of the boat, it was a thousand times worse. Many an experienced seaman made his first offering to Neptune on this occasion.

On the third day it grew calmer. The sea became smoother and we were able to open the hatches in order to air and dry the boat.

All the men of the off duty watch came on deck and stretched themselves out in the sun, seeking a much-needed relaxation.

Worn out and pale faced they appeared through the hatches; and hardly had they inhaled the fresh sea breeze before their beloved pipes were lighted.

As we met very few steamers on our present course, we set to work to give everything a good drying. All the wet articles that could not be dried down below were brought up into the air.

The whole deck was packed with beds, coverlets, clothes, and boots. The clothes were fastened securely to the deck rails, where they fluttered merrily in the wind, as if from a washing line. In between them the crew reposed in the strangest positions, sunning themselves like lizards. In order to increase the artificial ventilation of the rooms by means of a draught of air, wind-sails were hung up in all the hatches. With their jagged side wings they looked rather like the fins of a fish, and made the rounded green superstructure of the *Deutschland* look like the back of a fantastic, monster whale. We must truly have presented a strange spectacle.

No one was near, however, to notice it. We sighted one steamer only, whose smoke appeared towards evening on the horizon, and we were easily able to steer clear of her.

The spirits of the crew were excellent, as was shown by the merry warbling of the gramophone from the men's room.

In our mess-room, likewise, we enlivened the time with classical music, without which life on a U-Boat would not bear thinking of. Moreover, the monotonous part of our journey was now to begin. The fine weather continued, and we met with few encounters.

I find in my journal only the following notes:

"The dull period of our journey is commencing. The boat is making her way, rolling slightly, but bearing herself bravely. Now and then we go out of our way to avoid a steamer. For several days there is nothing to be seen; the gramophones play gaily, and everyone is in the best of humours. On the open sea we are entirely dependent on the weather for our comfort."

It was, as a matter of fact, the first moment that we had been able to breathe freely. Looking round on all sides one became almost incorporated with the everlasting sameness of the sea.

One day I was standing on the fore-deck. Near me Humke, our giant boatswain, squatted in the wooden scaffolding of the small central upper-deck under which we had snugly stored our lifeboat. Several lashings had been loosened during the stormy weather, and had to be repaired.

I had stood there for some time, gazing westward, my thoughts fixed on America, our destination.

Suddenly I took it into my head to broach the subject to the sturdy Humke. I asked him what he thought of our voyage to America in these, days of war. What were his impressions as to the object of our enterprise?

The rascal grinned broadly and replied:

"Why, to earn money, of course."

This reply was a little too summary for my taste, and I proceeded to explain to him the real significance of renewing our commercial relations with America in war time, in defiance of the English blockade. I then proceeded to make clear to him exactly what the blockade meant.

He grasped the idea quickly, and said:

"Well, now I understand what the English are after."

I went further, and explained to him as fully as I could the meaning and exigencies of an effective blockade, and was surprised at the directness of his answer, which expressed so naively and with such confidence the feelings of the people in the simple language of our sea-folk.

"Well, they won't get *us*, any'ow! And so there ain't no sense in the English blockade, as I can see!"

In the meantime several of the watch off duty had strolled up and gathered around to listen. There they stood, broad-legged, on the narrow deck of our little submarine in the middle of the Atlantic, a handful of sturdy, unabashed German seamen.

"Men," I said, "you have heard now the reason of our voyage, but

I will tell you something more. My good fellows, you have no idea what our cruise really signifies. Our gallant *Deutschland* is much more than a mere U-Boat merchant-trader. By her means we are bringing German goods to America; goods which the commercial jealousy and trickiness of the English have so far prevented from reaching that country. And this not only to injure Germany's exports, but in order to continue their gloomy fishing over yonder they do their utmost to harm American industry and commerce.

"That is all a thing of the past. We are seeing to that. But this is not all. The appearance of the first U-Boat trader is of far deeper significance. Without even a gun or torpedo on board, the *Deutschland* is revolutionising the entire methods of navigation, overseas trade and international rights, a revolution whose effects can hardly be fully realised as yet.

"How, in these days of warfare, have our armed U-Boats fared? We wanted to use them as a means to prevent this barbaric starvation blockade, which violates every right of humanity, and what did the English do? They armed their merchant-men and shot down every U-Boat that approached them with the object of sinking their contraband.

"That is what they call 'defending themselves.' And what is the result? We proceed to defend our skin and our U-Boats,—knowing that in every fishing vessel a 'Baralong' murderer lies in wait,—by sinking the armed English merchant ships without warning in order to save ourselves from being rammed or fired on.

"Thereupon the English shriek for help, and by reason of the existing conventions of sea warfare they win the Americans over to their side, for under the present laws of sea warfare there are no definite conditions laid down for U-Boats. We wish to maintain friendly relations with the great American people, and therefore give in. The Government which rewarded the 'Baralong' commanders has triumphed apparently, and the command goes forth: merchant ships are not to be sunk without warning.

"Then our *Deutschland* appears on the scenes, a U-Boat and merchantman combined. Now merchantmen must not be sunk without warning, and, moreover, the present laws of sea warfare contain no definite conditions for U-Boats. A U-Boat trader, however, that must be searched before sinking would be difficult to recognise, if still capable of submerging. For then the swiftest torpedo-boat is powerless.

"The English are caught in their own trap, for the *Deutschland* throws the whole one-sided interpretation of the rules of naval warfare on the rubbish heap. The weapon that was at first used against us must now speak in our favour.

"For the matter stands thus. If merchantmen—which can at the same time be U-Boats—may not be sunk without warning, then according to the laws and formalities of sea warfare the *Deutschland* has rendered the English blockade futile. For I should like to see the German U-Trader that would allow an English patrol vessel to approach near enough to examine her!

"Or supposing she is not searched. Then, in that case, merchant traders *can* be sunk without warning—English traders likewise. And thus the rights of warfare will be evenly balanced once more by means of a peaceful, unarmed U-Boat trader. And this, my men, is where the enormous significance of our *Deutschland* lies."

Thereupon I concluded my speech, which was by far the longest I had ever made.

★★★★★★

The fine weather still continued. The barometer remained steady, the air was dry and clear. We were gradually approaching the latitudes in which fine weather is the rule at that time of the year. The warmth of the sun's rays began to be felt, and our thoughts turned towards refreshment.

This was provided us by our "wave-bath," a discovery of the observation engineer, Herr Kiszling, who otherwise showed no interest in anything but his beloved engines. For these he was full of the most touching and undeviating solicitude. Often, during a heavy sea, when all the deck hatches were closed, he would suddenly appear through the conning-hatch and push hastily through into the "bath-tank," regardless of the exigencies of higher navigation in process there.

When the officer on duty looked round, annoyed at the disturbance, there was our sturdy Kiszling, in his oldest oilskins, leaning over the side of the dripping deck—filled with care for the welfare of his engines, trying to get a glimpse of the exhaust. At the same time he must see if the ignition was working properly, if the heartbeats of his engines were carrying out their functions, and if the explosions were quite regular. He was wrapped up in his beloved machinery and lived on its rhythmical music. He noticed at once the least irregularity in its working, and spared no trouble in getting to the bottom of it.

It must have been during one of these special tours of his, which were by no means without danger, over the rounded slippery side-deck, that the inspiration came to him. In brief, he opened to us the joyful possibility of the "wave-bath."

In order to understand this, it is first necessary to know the construction of the upper part of the *Deutschland*. Above the cylindrical hull, on the sides of which are the submersion tanks and oil bunkers, rises the outer ship, which gives the vessel its real ship form.

In this upper part of the outer ship, the so-called "outer tanks" are placed which, when the ship is laden, are always flooded, as water and air may penetrate to their interior by numerous openings, holes and slits, in order that a rapid filling and emptying may be achieved. The "outer tanks," therefore, have no connection with the floating capacity of the boat; they are only the result of the outer construction which above water does not follow the line of the heavy hull and tanks. In spite of their relatively unimportant functions the "outer tanks" must, of course, be accessible from the upper parts of the vessel. This is made possible by large movable steel lids and by ladders on the upper surface of the deck. Standing on the so-called tank-deck, therefore, you have a slight elevation to the upper deck surface. The sea water is continually rushing into these big spaces during the voyage. You have only to climb in through the opened plate lids to enjoy an absolutely safe and delightful sea-water bath.

We did not fail to put this into practice pretty often, and found our bath delightful. There was only one drawback to the business. If, for instance, you entered the sea-water bath for the first time, soon after the boat had risen to the surface, you found yourself not in sea-water, but in an oil bath!

The bunkers, as a matter of fact, never hold quite tight, especially after a long strain of travelling, and so it often happens that as the boat rises to the surface a curious layer of oil breaks through before she reaches the top. This layer of oil is then to be found in the "bath tank," on the lids of the hatches and on deck. Inside the "outer tanks "it naturally remains on the surface of the water, for there it is not able to mix and disperse quickly. It generally remains there a day, sometimes longer, till the oily water is drained off and replaced by new water again. The unlucky man, therefore, who took a bath during this period, emerged but little refreshed and with a shiny nickel-coated skin. This metamorphosis, as can be imagined, caused great amusement among the crew.

★★★★★★

The fine weather now was very favourable for submerging tests, which were made practically every day. Everything worked perfectly smoothly, and we felt we could safely approach the American coast and submerge within the three-mile zone.

During one of these submerging tests a wonderful and fairy-like spectacle was presented to us. I had caused the boat to be steered so that the conning-tower lay nearly two fathoms under water. Above, the sun shone brightly and filled the deeps with radiant light. The water was lit by many colours. Around us the sea was of brightest azure blue of an almost dazzling clearness, and transparent as glass. From the window of the conning-tower I could see the whole length of the boat, round which rose twinkling air bubbles, like pearls. In strange, fantastic distinctness the deck lay stretched out before me, even the furthest bow end was visible. Further ahead was a dim-coloured twilight. It seemed as if the bow of the boat was gliding silently through a wall of opal green, which opened up as she moved, and broke into a dazzling radiant-coloured transparency of light.

We were spellbound at this wonderful sight, and the strangeness of the effect was increased by the jelly-fish as they floated through the transparent blue and were caught in the wires of the deck rails, where they shimmered first rose colour, then pale yellow, changing slowly to purple.

We were not able at that slight depth to observe any fish.

The next day a little incident occurred which afforded us much amusement, though it turned out rather differently from what we had expected.

My ambition was to follow in the tracks of my comrades of the merchant service and the navy, who had disguised their ships from the enemy by painting and clever alterations in their outward structure.

During the previous fine spell of weather we had made a wonderful trap for steamers, in order to disguise our identity as a U-Boat from ships passing in the distance. We had rigged up a funnel out of some sail-cloth, which could be fixed to the periscope with several wire rings, till it rose proudly in the air.

The conning-tower was also provided with a covering of sail-cloth to make it resemble the upper middle deck of a small trading vessel.

Thus, ready for all emergencies, we travelled on in the brilliant sunshine, till at 7.30 in the evening a steamer appeared in the distance to starboard. We soon realised that she must pass quite near to us if we continued on our present course. We held aloof from her therefore and proceeded to try the effects of our disguise.

The "funnel" is fixed up on to the periscope and rises proudly erect in the wind. In order to give it a more realistic appearance we burn some cotton waste steeped in oil at its base. Then the conning-tower disappears under the rather flattering "middle deck."

But the disobliging cotton-wool only smoulders horribly and refuses to give out any smoke. Everyone stands round puffing out their cheeks, but in vain, till the wireless operator, a shrewd Berliner, fetches an air-pump, which produces a powerful glow in our imaginary boiler. A cheer greets his handiwork, and sure enough from the upper edge of the "funnel "a delicate cloud of smoke appears, only to vanish immediately into thin air!

Laughing, we decide to continue on our way smokeless, when up comes the boatswain, Humke, with a jam-pot full of tar. The air-pump is again brought into play, and at last our funnel can really be said to smoke!

The effect is certainly startling. For the steamer suddenly alters her course and bears straight down on us!

This is not exactly our intention. The masts are immediately hauled down and everything cleared for submerging; the middle deck disappears, and with a deep bow our beautiful funnel falls together in a heap.

No sooner does the steamer observe this than she is seized with wild amazement and horror. She turns round again abruptly and seeks flight, puffing out thick black clouds of smoke which we eye not without a certain feeling of envy.

Once more we raise our indefatigable funnel. The masts are lifted high, and while the steamer hastens away in wildest flight we stand and laugh till the tears come.

The situation was really humorous beyond description.

Our beautiful disguise, which was to screen us from observation, had been the very means of bringing the gallant steamer's attention to bear upon us. She obviously took us for a wreck, or some ship in distress, and approached probably with the best intentions, to find herself face to face with the devilish tricks of one of those rascally submarines.

What must the people on board have thought when they had recovered from the first effects of the shock? Undoubtedly they would pride themselves greatly on having escaped so cleverly this new piece of "piratical" cunning.

And we should have been so proud if our disguise had only worked a little better! We were not discouraged, however, but set to work to improve on our invention, with the result that two days later we steamed by an approaching vessel unrecognised under our own powerful smoke!

CHAPTER 8

The Inferno

June comes gradually to an end, and with it unfortunately the fine weather. A rising swell from the S.W. and the absence of the current which we had expected to help us along indicates a storm centre in the south, diverting the course of the Gulf Stream. Thus we travel on throughout another day. Towards evening the atmosphere becomes close and heavy and the sun sinks slowly in a misty blood-red veil.

The sky grows threatening and overcast; there is brilliant sheet lightning, while the ever-increasing closeness of the atmosphere announces the near vicinity of the Gulf Stream. During the night masses of heavy thunder-clouds roll up, the wind rises on every side, and the wildness of the running seas increases, till steer Lag becomes noticeably difficult.

Measurements record an increase in the water temperature, which finally rises up to 82½ degrees Fahrenheit. Now we are in the Gulf Stream, whose periphery is marked in the air above by a fiery crown of heavy tropical thunder-clouds.

Vivid sea phosphorescence and strong atmospherical disturbances are also accompanying sign of the presence of the Stream. This is noticeable from our wireless apparatus, which is strongly-affected by the heavy electrical conditions of the atmosphere. Hitherto it has kept us faithfully in touch with the army bulletins from the Nauen station.

The phosphorescence of the waters makes observation very difficult. One's eyes are blinded and observation made difficult by the continuous sparkling of the surface of the sea in the blackness of the night. This state of things is far from pleasant, for we are now approaching a zone where many steamer tracks cross each other, and double precautions are necessary.

Added to this, the foulness of the weather increases. Heavy seas spring up, and a storm of hail beats down on the deck. Over the foaming whipped-up waves a wind of strength 11 to 12 is blowing.

All around over the boiling sea hang heavy black balls of clouds, from which a pale yellow light darts out incessantly—regular broadsides of lightning. Then suddenly all is enveloped in blackest night again, while at times the whole boat and the surrounding water are lit up by flashes of greenish light, in which every detail shows up with startling distinctness. . . .

The whole air is filled with tumultuous uproar, and overhead the thunder crashes continuously. We are approaching the centre of the storm. The boat is surrounded by an unearthly storm-world. It is as if the end of all things had come. . . .

Suddenly the headlights of a big steamer rise up behind us. In the darkness of the night we are able to avoid her without difficulty. Like a shining vision she disappears in the distance. She is a passenger steamer who, judging by her course, has come from the Mediterranean. I must confess we watched her row of lights with a feeling of envy, till rain and darkness swallowed her up from sight again.

The next day the weather reaches its worst stage. Hurricane-like gusts of wind sweep all around. The air is filled with continuous froth. The water no longer falls in drops, but in cascades—walls of water pour down, lashing our faces and hands painfully. The air is so thick that one can no longer see through it. In order to observe anything ever so faintly, a small piece of glass has to be held in front of the eyes, with the result that a little foaming torrent rolls from the pane on to your sleeves.

The boat travels with extreme difficulty in the roaring sea. She is tossed here and there by the waves till every joint creaks and groans. Sometimes she heels over so heavily that it is almost impossible to hold on with one free hand only, to the parapet of the "bath-tank."

It is an Inferno.

But this is nothing to the hell down below, particularly in the engine room.

Owing to the heavy seas all the hatches are of necessity closed; even the conning-tower hatch can only be opened occasionally. Two great ventilation machines are working unceasingly, it is true. But the fresh air that they draw from the ventilation shaft, which is carefully protected from the breakers, is immediately swallowed up by the greedy Diesel engines. These hungry, ungrateful monsters only give off heat in return, heavy over-bearing heat impregnated with horrible oil vapour, which is then swept by the ventilators throughout all the other compartments. Such ventilation can no longer be of a refreshing nature.

The air in the boat on this account has become overwhelmingly laden with moisture. It is almost an impossibility to breathe, and one awaits with resignation, or desperate gaiety, the moment when one really will be forced to join the fishes. In the closed-up body of the ship every object is covered in steaming water which again evaporates in the heat, till everything is soaked through and streaming. All the drawers and cupboard doors swell and stick fast, and added to this the wet clothes from the watchers in the conning-tower are spread out over the whole boat.

It is impossible to give any idea of the state of the temperature that then reigned in the boat. In the Gulf Stream the outside temperature was 82 degrees Fahrenheit, so extraordinarily warm was the water around us. Fresh air no longer penetrated, and in the engine-room the two six-cylinder combustion engines hammered on in ceaseless rhythm. . . . A choking cloud of heat and oil vapour issued from the engines and spread through every part of the boat.

The temperature rose gradually in these days to 127 degrees Fahrenheit.

And in such an inferno men lived and worked. Groaning, the naked off-duty watch rolled about in their cabins. Sleep was out of the question. When one of them was just dropping off into a heavy stupor he would be awakened to fresh misery by the perspiration running in drops from his forehead into his eyes.

It was almost a relief when the eight hours' rest was over and the watchmen were called once more into the control-room or the engine-room.

Then the martyrdom recommenced. Clad only in shirt and trousers the men stood at their posts, a cloth wrapped round their foreheads to keep the perspiration out of their eyes. The blood glowed and rushed in their temples-fever was in their veins. It was only by the greatest strength of will that they were able to force their streaming bodies to perform their allotted duties, and to keep going during the four hours' watch.

But how long could this state of things be expected to last?

During these days I kept no journal, and can only find the following note: "If the temperature rises any higher the men in the engine-room will not be able to stand it any longer."

They did stand it, however,—they kept going like heroes, doing their work in spite of exhaustion, till at last the storm centre lay behind us, the weather cleared up, the sun broke through the clouds, and the dropping of the sea made it possible to open the hatches once more.

Then they climbed up out of their inferno, pale, covered with dirt and oil, and rejoiced in the sun as if they had never seen it before.

CHAPTER 9

America

While crossing the Atlantic we had avoided approaching steamers by slightly altering our course. We had even risked being noticed on one or two occasions, but during the last days of our voyage we submerged directly a cloud of smoke appeared on the horizon. On no account must we be observed when approaching the coast, as we had to reckon with the presence of enemy warships.

On the 8th July we guessed by the colour of the water that we could not be far from our goal.

In the course of the afternoon I conferred with my officers as to the navigation of Cape Henry, the southernmost of the two headlands which form the entrance to the roadstead of Hampton Road and Chesapeake Bay.

My idea was to await daybreak at about ten knots out from the American territorial waters in order to discover whether any enemy measures had been taken. If by any chance news of our voyage had leaked out, we should certainly have to reckon with such enemy influences.

Krapohl, on the other hand, was for getting in as near the coast as possible under cover of the night, and Eyring was of the same opinion.

Both plans had their fors and againsts, and eventually I decided to continue our way carefully in the twilight, and wait to see what the weather conditions would be.

No sooner was our decision made than a stiff breeze from the south-west sprang up which cleared our range of vision considerably. At the same time, however, the boat started rolling in a very disagreeable manner, in the stiff, choppy sea that had risen with the breeze. We decided, therefore, to follow the direction of the lights on Cape

Henry and Cape Charles through the night.

We proceeded on our course, till not long after a pale light flashed out suddenly on the horizon, then disappeared again.

This was the glow of the flashlights on Cape Henry—the first greeting from America.

Suddenly a white light shone out in the distance to starboard, disappeared, and then flared out again. It was immediately succeeded by a white light on our port side, which, however, continued to shine steadily.

We looked at each other.

What the blazes did this mean? It looked uncommonly like darkened warships making flashlight signals to each other. In any case, it meant a devilish sharp look out on our part.

At half-speed, submerged up to the conning-tower, every man at his station, we crept nearer, maintaining the closest observation, our glasses boring their way through the darkness.

It was not long before we discovered that the steady light proceeded from a harmless outgoing steamer, which was already hurrying away at some distance behind us. Soon after we were able to make out from the place whence the flickering light had appeared, the outlines of the sail of a three-masted schooner, which like many coast steamers was travelling without side-lights, and only showing a white light at her stern from time to time. This was what we had taken for the signalling of warships.

Much relieved, I let the engines go full speed ahead, and soon we hove in full sight of the steady flare from Cape Henry, while the quivering lights of Cape Charles grew clearer and clearer on the horizon. Now we knew that we had steered correctly. The entrance between the two headlands lay before us.

The lights were now plainly visible. With an indescribable feeling in my heart I greeted the flare from Cape Charles, which shone out in the surrounding darkness a silent but sure sign that over yonder, after our long and dangerous journey, was firm land again, that over yonder lay our goal—mighty America.

We passed now by the various light buoys of the roadstead, and the familiar ringing of the siren buoy nearby, which I had heard on former voyages, assured my ears as well as my eyes that we were near *terra firma*.

After we had passed the bell buoy we rose fully to the surface. The lights of several passenger steamers were visible, but they did not discover us as we were travelling with darkened lights. At last we reached the territorial waters off Cape Henry.

This was on the 8th July at 11.30 p.m.

Once inside the territorial waters we started our lights and proceeded steadily on our way through the roadstead between the capes, till we made out the red and white headlights of a pilot steamer ahead of us.

We stopped and showed the customary blue light, whereupon the pilot steamer brought her searchlight to bear upon us, and not recognising the outlines of a steamer, approached cautiously.

She held us for some time under her searchlight, whose rays played continuously over the low deck and conning-tower of the *Deutschland*. The unexpected appearance of our boat seemed so to have bewildered the gallant captain, that it was some time before he called out to us through the speaking trumpet: "Where are you bound for?"

On our replying "Newport News," he asked the name of our ship. We gave the name, but it was necessary to repeat it twice before he grasped the real nature of this strange visitor. Thereupon there must have been a great sensation on board the pilot steamer.

Then a boat approached us swiftly, and the pilot climbed up the rounded hull of the *Deutschland* on to her deck and greeted us with the following hearty words:

"I'll be damned; so here she is!"

Then he shook hands heartily with us again and expressed his pleasure at being the first American to welcome the *Deutschland* to the land of liberty.

I asked him immediately if he had had any idea that we were expected. To my surprise and delight, I learnt that for the last few, days a tug had been awaiting our arrival between the capes.

We started off therefore with our trusty pilot in search of her.

In the meanwhile the incoming steamers had discovered the nature of this curious new arrival, and lit us up on all sides with their searchlights.

. Thus our arrival in American waters was rather in the nature of a weird nocturne.

The search for our tug-boat was, however, by no means an easy matter in the darkness. We cruised around for some time till at last, after two hours, we found her.

It was the tug *Timmins*, under the command of Captain Hinsch of the North German Lloyd.

Great was his delight, for the gallant captain, whose steamer, the *Neckar,"* had lain at Baltimore since the beginning of the war, had been waiting nearly ten days for us between the capes. Our long delay had filled him with distress as to our possible fate.

Now, however, he was delighted to see his long-expected *protégé* safe and sound before his eyes. He communicated to us thereupon the order to proceed to Baltimore instead of Newport News, where everything was already prepared for our arrival.

We parted therefore from our honest pilot, and travelled on, accompanied by the *Timmins*, into Chesapeake Bay, after proudly hoisting the German flag which had not fluttered over these waters since the arrival of the *Eitel Friedrich* in front of Hampton Road.

In this manner we entered the bay in the grey morning light. Our course became by degrees a triumphal procession. All the American and neutral steamers that met us greeted us with prolonged tootings from pipes and sirens. One English steamer only passed by us in poisonous silence, while our black, white and red flag fluttered proudly in the wind before her eyes.

Captain Hinsch, moreover, in his tug, took devilish care that the Englishman should not by chance run too close in by the rudder and ram us by mistake!

The gallant *Timmins* was useful to us in other ways. Our only means of responding to the greetings of the various steamers was by driving the siren by means of our precious compressed air. This would have gradually become an expensive game, and so the *Timmins* undertook to return thanks for us with her hoarse steam whistle.

The further we advanced into the bay the wilder grew the noise . We rejoiced from the depths of our hearts at these signs of sympathy with us and our cruise on the part of the Americans.

Towards four o'clock in the afternoon the *Timmins* was able to come up alongside and handed up to us—a block of ice! A couple of bottles of champagne were quickly cooled, and proudly we toasted the successful arrival of the *Deutschland* in America, our one regret in connection with this performance being that our faithful Hinsch only came in for the corks which flew on board the tug.

Only those who can realise what it means to have lived day after day in a temperature of 127½ degrees Fahrenheit will fully appreciate the joy of that first cool iced drink.

The news of our arrival must have spread with extraordinary rapidity, for to our no small surprise, hours before we reached Baltimore,

boats came out to meet us with reporters and cinematograph opera-
tors on board.

Although it was growing dusk we were fairly bombarded, and we
should probably have had to run the gauntlet of a still greater stream
of questions and calls if the weather-god of Chesapeake Bay had not
come hospitably to the rescue and ensured us a little breathing space. A
heavy storm arose suddenly, and the stream of questions was quenched
by a stream of rain which fell refreshingly down upon us sunburnt
seafarers. Meanwhile through the fast approaching evening the *Deutschland*, accompanied by the faithful *Timmins*, travelled on once more
silent and lonely towards her goal.

At 11 p.m. we drew in to the Baltimore quarantine station, and for
the first time our anchor struck American ground.

The *U Deutschland* had arrived.

CHAPTER 10

Baltimore

Our first glance the following morning fell on the stout little *Timmins*, who had moored up along-side. There she lay, the faithful soul— and mounted guard over us.

Shortly after, at five o'clock, the doctor of the quarantine station came along. I gave him up our health certificate, which had been carefully made out for us on 13th June by Mr. William Thomas Fee, the American Consul at Bremen. The doctor then examined the boat, and after mustering the crew set us free, and ended up by giving three cheers for the *Deutschland* and her crew.

The anchor was hauled up, and we travelled under the guidance of *Timmins* towards our wharf and resting-place at Locust Point.

Never before, surely, has a boat travelled under such conditions as now fell to our lot, guarded jealously by our *Timmins* and surrounded by a crowd of boats specially hired by the various film companies. On each boat five or six men stood ready with their cameras, and tried to rouse us to suitable cinematograph poses by chaffing remarks.

"Show your face, Cap!"

"Turn your head round!"

"Wave your hand!" These and similar cries arose on every side, while the fellows pushed and shoved and shouted like madmen.

I stood in the conning-tower and looked to right and left, waved both hands, and had no need to force a laugh, for the wild movements of the film hunters were indescribably funny.

Thus in the merriest of moods we reached our resting-place at Locust Point.

Here our Captain Hinsch had spent weeks in making all ready for us. The *Deutschland* found such a safe harbour, and was so protected by booms and netting from the approach of any strange vessel, that according to all human calculations nothing could possibly happen to her.

We lay inside a wooden pier built out into the stream, under cover of a great shed, in which our destined cargo was already piled up in waiting for us. The situation lay so apart that the connection of the pier with the nearest good road must be first explained.

The whole position was shut off from the land by a big trench and a steel wire fencing. In the stream itself the *Deutschland* was protected by the pier and the North German Lloyd steamer *Neckar*, which had lain at Baltimore since the beginning of the war and now served us as a place of residence, from which we could watch over our boat.

On the other side, surrounding the *Deutschland*, a regular network of heavy beams stretched out, with thick nets which reached to the bottom of the water, so that it would be impossible even for a diver to get at the boat. Moreover, day and night patrol-boats guarded the spot, among them the *Timmins*, which lit up the surrounding neighbourhood with her little searchlight all night long.

Many amusing incidents occurred in connection with this.

In order that the unloading and reloading of the *Deutschland* should proceed without observation, yet another high palisading had been erected round the warehouse sheds which prohibited the least view of the ship and loading place.

The only spot from which a glimpse of the wonderful boat, even at some distance, could be obtained, was from a pile-driver which was anchored in the stream, and which was immediately besieged by newspaper reporters as a place of observation. Here they nested, holding us well in sight, and keeping watch with the utmost regularity. Day and night two men sat there continuously, perched high on the slender scaffolding of the pile-driver, in sacrificial practice of their calling!

We were also at our posts. And at night, during the change of watch yonder on the pile-driver, the searchlight operator of the *Timmins* had his bit of fun by enveloping the reporters in beams of light and thus politely "lightening their darkness" and assisting them in their difficult task. As they climbed cautiously down from the scaffolding they were each singled out by a beam of light, one after the other, like spiders with a pocket lamp.

For the rest the gallant Captain Hinsch had seen to everything, from our reception and safe guidance down to the provision for our wants on board the *Neckar*.

From this steamer only a favoured few were allowed a sight of the *Deutschland*, and that only from the outside. A visit to the boat was strictly forbidden.

For her own sake we should have been glad and proud to show our wonderful boat to everyone. For fear, however, of the risk of an attack, which might easily arise on the German U-Boat trader if everyone had been allowed an inspection, we dared not depart from our instructions in this respect. And thus hundreds of Americans who had come great distances, even from the west, in their motorcars, were obliged, much to our regret, to depart without having achieved their object.

The cinematograph companies, however, did not go away entirely empty-handed. I granted their wish to immortalise the crew of the *Deutschland* on her first touching on American soil, and all of us were photographed in a group on deck.

My first journey through the town resembled a triumphal entry. The car was obliged to pull up continually. Everyone tried to shake me by the hand and pour out their congratulations.

During the first few days in Baltimore I became simply an obstruction to the traffic.

In this manner we proceeded slowly to the North German Lloyd agency, which was surrounded by crowds of people.

The next step was to go through the necessary Custom House formalities. I made my way therefore to the Customs House authorities, and got through the usual examination; I was received on all sides in the most hearty and friendly manner.

Then I went back to the agency and devoted all my sailor-like abilities to the Press. I stood in the office of the North German Lloyd agency behind the barrier of the booking bureau, on the other side of which a huge crowd was pressing. I was quite alone, and had to hold my own against hundreds of men and women, who each had some particular question to put, from the most insignificant personalities up to the highest region of politics.

One lady called out:

"Do tell me, Captain, what it is like in a submarine?" Another asked with deep sympathy, "I say, is it true that in Germany the babies are starving for want of milk?" While a gentleman of extremely well-fed appearance showed his interest by the question, "Say, Captain, what do you live on?"

I was also frequently asked: "What about the Emperor's message you've brought over for Mr. Wilson?" To which I could give as little information as to the question, "When do you think of leaving Baltimore again?"

To all these and a hundred other questions I was obliged to make answer. I stood there like a breakwater, the tide swirling round me, creeping higher and higher, till my conscious self was almost swallowed up, only on the following day to reappear in bits in endless Press notices all over the world.

Meanwhile my body proceeded, somewhat fatigued, to the German club, where we had been invited to celebrate our arrival at a purely German gathering, during which our thoughts flew back with pride and love to the struggling Fatherland over yonder.

★★★★★★

The following days were in the nature of a continuous festivity for us. Only those who know American hospitality and enthusiasm can form any idea of the cordiality that greeted us on all sides.

The people went quite mad over us, and it did one's heart good to see what genuine sympathy all the Americans showed over our journey and safe arrival, and to hear how warmly they expressed their feelings on the subject.

Everywhere we went we were enthusiastically received. They shook us by the hand, sang the "Watch on the Rhine," and expressed their appreciation by eloquent ovations. Invitations rained down on officers and men, parties and feasts were held in our honour, and on one occasion, when my two officers of the watch, who were walking with a friend in some public gardens, became recognised, the concert music suddenly stopped, a searchlight was flashed on to them, and amidst general acclamation the band struck up the "Watch on the Rhine" and the American National Anthem.

While the general public of all ranks and classes thus showed their appreciation, the American Government were dealing with the official side of the question as to whether our boat was to be regarded as a merchantman pure and simple, or whether, in accordance with the urgent protests of the English and French ambassadors, she would, in her character of submarine alone, be regarded as a war vessel.

On the 12th July a Government Commission, consisting of three American marine officers, came from Washington to inspect our *Deutschland* thoroughly. As there was no sign of armament, or arrangements for bringing any such on board, we were quite ready to show them over everything.

After a three hours' inspection, during which every compartment and comer were examined, and which cost the Commission officers many a drop of perspiration during the crawling around in the glowing heat of the boat, the Commission confirmed the purely mercantile character of the *U Deutschland*.

They were at no pains to conceal their admiration for the ingenious construction of the whole boat, and expressed particularly the staggering impression of bewilderment which the complicated mechanism of all the works had made upon them.

In honour of the whole crew a German festival was started by the many German-Americans of Baltimore, in aid of the Red Cross. This was celebrated in Canstätter Park, a great public park near Baltimore, with shooting galleries, sausage stalls, open stage, dancing ground, and other forms of amusement in the open air. I must say our men stood this test on land as well as they had that on the water. They acquitted themselves bravely throughout this homage and were not awkward. When dancing began they chose their partners without hesitation, and a couple of smart fellows even danced with the ladies who had got up the *fête*, as if they had been used to it all their lives.

★★★★★★

On the 20th July the *Deutschland* received a visit from the German ambassador, Count Bernstorff, who had come with several gentlemen from the summer residence of the embassy to Baltimore.

We showed them over our gallant boat with pride, although an inspection in the midst of the embarkation of her cargo and in the intense heat was by no means an entirely delightful one.

On the evening of the same day, there was an official dinner given by the Mayor of Baltimore, in honour of the visit of the German embassy, preceded by a small luncheon party at the Germania Club House.

The dinner given by the mayor—a most amiable man—was of an exclusively political character, and was only attended by politicians and officials. There was a long succession of excellent courses and wines, and according to American custom, with the appearance of the endless drinks at the close of it, many speeches were made in which the arrival of the *Deutschland* in America, and its importance in connection with Baltimore and German-American friendship, were celebrated.

Then the municipal band appeared in the town gardens and played the "Watch on the Rhine" and the American hymn, while the German and American flags were crossed.

This was a pleasing symbol of friendship and understanding between the two peoples whose interests both lay in the freedom of the seas.

★★★★★★

While all these festivities were in progress, which took up nearly all our evenings, the unloading of our boat had been completed, and the embarkation begun.

This was quite a special chapter in itself. Messrs. P. H. L. and H. G. Hilken, the representatives of the North German Lloyd at Baltimore, had done everything in their power to make this extremely delicate part of our task as easy and safe as possible for us.

They had not only acquired, on the quiet, all the goods for our return cargo, and had them taken to the sheds ready for loading—it was a jolly fine stock, too, and many who saw it wondered how on earth such a quantity of goods could ever be stored away on a U-Boat—but they had even procured the necessary and specially adapted loading and stocking personnel—gangs of lightermen and dockers.

Much of the work on the boat and wharf was undertaken by niggers, who were closely watched for the least sign of observation powers or other dangerous faculties. Moreover, the niggers were closely searched each time before they commenced work, and obliged to strip entirely, in order to secure the boat against any attack.

The unloading was completed without any further difficulties.

The embarkation, however, was a more difficult matter. For this careful calculations on the part of our expert submarine embarkation specialist, shipping engineer, Prusse, of the Germania dock, were first necessary. Every pound of the varying weights and sizes of the goods to be loaded had to be reckoned up before being stowed in the space particularly appointed for them, in order to prevent an unequal trimming of the boat.

An absolutely exact storing was necessary, inasmuch as the whole loading space was very limited, and every box and sack must be held firmly in its position. Otherwise the most unpleasant occurrences might arise, either during a storm, by sudden submersions at a steep angle, or any other incidents, which might seriously impede our navigation.

An embarkation of this kind therefore was bound to be a lengthy affair.

The whole cargo, sacks and boxes, had to be carried by hand by the niggers through the narrow hatchways. The goods had first to be weighed, piece by piece, each separately—the weighing-inspector taking notes meanwhile and calling out the number of weights, which were then carefully indexed.

This indexing was part of a specially thought-out plan, according to which the whole packing was exactly carried out, and the accuracy of this plan was then tested by a submersion and boat-trimming test, for which our mooring-place had just sufficient depth of water.

For this test the crew all took up their submerging stations, the submersion tanks were slowly opened and the boat flooded with just sufficient water to make her float, the conning-tower hatch still remaining above the surface.

In this way the hull of the boat is made to oscillate by means of the different water loads of the two trimming tanks, and from this one can judge if the balance of the boat is properly adjusted. If after this it is found necessary to alter the weights, the cargo is moved accordingly. One last submerging and trimming test must then follow, in order to make sure that the loading of the whole boat agrees in every detail.

Thus her two thousand tons are brought into perfect adjustment in the fluctuating displacement of the water.

CHAPTER 11

The Departure From Baltimore

Above the description of our return voyage I should like to put as a motto what the London *Morning Post* of 18th July wrote regarding the attitude of the English Government towards the *Deutschland*.

"The *Deutschland*, in view of her peculiar U-Boat qualities, will be considered as a war vessel, and be treated as such.

"The warships of the Allies will therefore make every effort to discover the boat outside American territorial waters, and to sink her without warning."

Thus ran a cablegram which reached America from London on the 19th July. Thus we ourselves read it in a copy of the *Morning Post* which was sent to us at the end of July. There was at least one advantage, that we knew exactly what we had to expect.

Never has the English point of view been so displayed in all its brutality.

We had no torpedo tubes, no guns on board, not the smallest means of attack. We had not even weapons of defence which are always allowed on every English merchant ship. The most powerful of the neutral states had moreover openly recognised the *Deutschland* as a mere trading vessel, and yet we were to be sunk without warning!

We knew, therefore, what lay before us.

It was already known that eight enemy warships with patrol boats and nets were waiting in front of Chesapeake Bay in order to attack us directly we quitted American territorial waters, and to blow us up like blind fish, with mines.

Foresight was therefore urgently impelled on us, and our only course was, with true U-Boat craftiness, to slip through somehow.

We remembered, moreover, how we had already once succeeded in getting the best of the English and French efforts. Our running of the English blockade in Europe had certainly been by no means a smooth pleasure trip.

Nothing had caused us greater amusement than the news of the delightful announcement made by Captain Gaunt of the English consulate in New York when the first rumour was heard of the voyage of a U-Boat to America. His reassuring words to the English public were: "It is impossible to send a U-Boat to America. And even if the Germans did send one we should soon catch her. A big submarine leaves a track of oil and machine dirt on the surface of the waters in her wake. Our fast cruisers would be able to follow these tracks and catch the boat for a dead certainty."

Captain Gaunt is the expert on affairs of navigation at the Consulate, and ought to know.

All we had to do, therefore, was to see to it that their second "catch" was as much of a "dead certainty" as the first.

At last the 1st of August arrived. We had taken a hearty leave everywhere, completed all formalities with the authorities, and were ready for sea and for our rendezvous with the gentlemen in front of the bay.

Our departure was delayed, as we were obliged to wait for the high tide, in order to get from the Patapsco River on which Baltimore is situated, across the intervening muddy bar out into Chesapeake Bay. The water rose very slowly during the day, as a north wind was blowing and prevented the tide in the long inlet from rising up quite as far as Baltimore.

We waited excitedly for the rising of the water, and at last, at five o'clock in the afternoon, the moment arrived. The ropes were cast off, the closely packed attendant boats made way, and the *Deutschland* pushed majestically off from the pier into the fairway. The tug *Timmins* ran alongside of us like a faithful sheepdog, snarling at the many big and small boats full of reporters and cinema people, if they approached too closely.

There was nothing to fear. The harbour police boat from Baltimore had been very kindly lent us, and the Customs boat from Maryland had received instructions to accompany us as far as the boundary line of their beat permitted.

Hundreds of people stood on the banks of the Patapsco River, waving and cheering us incessantly as we departed, and in the harbour all the tugs hooted with the full blast of their sirens and hooters, while the steamers dipped their flags and tooted. It was an indescribable uproar. We knew as we travelled on that the thoughts and blessings of countless hearts throughout mighty America accompanied us, and anxiously awaited the moment which should bring them the certainty of our lucky escape out yonder.

As soon as we got into the fairway with the engines going at full speed, our attendants gradually fell behind. Even *Timmins* had enough to do to keep up with us. We noticed with pleasure how slowly all the American boats travelled; the cheers grew weaker and weaker, the number of boats ever smaller, and at last only the Customs' cutter remained. When towards seven o'clock she also dropped off, we should have been alone with *Timmins* but for one uncanny follower who was not so easy to shake off. She was a smart grey boat with pointed nose and flat short stern, a regular first-class racing boat which, so rumour said, had an 80 horse-power and could do her 22 knots. She appeared to have been hired during the last ten days by a man who paid the round sum of 200 dollars a day—by which it may be gathered how highly he valued this chance of a bit of sport in running a race with the *Deutschland.* . . . . By 10 p.m. a fairly roughish sea had risen. The lights of the racing boat dropped more and more behind, and at grey dawn the following morning the sea was empty—the racer had turned back home.

In her place, however, a whole lot of fishing trawlers appeared ahead of us in the dim morning light, which made us fear that even here in neutral waters we might run into a regular trap.

Cheers and hand-waving from the vessels soon showed us our happy mistake; they were a party of American Press representatives who, together with a number of admirers and friends of the *Deutschland*, had refused to miss the opportunity afforded by a night voyage of giving our boat a farewell greeting at a distance of some fifty miles from Baltimore.

One steamer after the other glided by, and the next morning by six o'clock we were in sufficiently free water to make our first submerging test. I wanted to get the boat and crew firmly in hand again after our prolonged stay on land—purely on account of the "dead certainty" of that "catch."

We therefore made our first trial, and everything went swimmingly. The *Timmins* stood by and Captain Hinsch told me later that it was a marvellous sight as the *Deutschland* dived in perfect silence, only to reappear again a few minutes later like a flash, her bow foaming, above the water.

The submersion worked perfectly likewise. After this, in order to see if everything was in working order, I gave the command for the boat to come to rest on the bottom at a spot which, according to the map, should have had a depth of 16½ fathoms.

Once more all is still. The daylight fades; the well-known singing and seething of the submersion valves sounds in our ears. The gauge in the conning-tower registers 11 fathoms, 13 fathoms; the power is lessened; 16½ fathoms appears, and I await the gentle impact with which the boat shall touch on the ground. . . .

Nothing of the kind happens.

Instead of this the hand moves round on its dial to 17½, 18, 19 fathoms. I tap my finger on the glass—quite all right, the hand is just turning to 20. "What in the name of fortune's the matter?" I think to myself, and take up the map.

Yes, 16½ fathoms are marked there and we had taken exact bearings up above. . . . Nevertheless, we continue to sink. Twenty-two fathoms are registered on the dial plate.

This is too absurd. I call down to the control-room and receive the comforting reply that on their big depth gauge also, "22 fathoms have been registered and passed. Our gauges coincide therefore.

This, however, does not prevent the boat from sinking.

The men in the control-room look at each other. . . .

It is a ridiculous situation, to be sinking in this confounded silence into the Unknown and not to be able to see anything but the everlasting backward jerking of that treacherous hand on the white dial. . . .

In the conning-tower it is no different. I glance distractedly backwards and forwards from the map to the gauge.

Meanwhile the boat sinks deeper and deeper; 24 fathoms have gone by. . . . The hand is moving towards 27. . . . I am just thinking that the deeps of Chesapeake Bay must come to an end somewhere, and that we can hardly be sinking into groundlessness . . . when suddenly, without the least shock, the boat comes to a halt at a depth of 27½ fathoms.

I scrambled down to the control-room and took counsel with Klees and the two officers of the watch.

It could only be that we had struck a hole which was not marked on the map. Well, this was nothing serious, after all. Whether we had to rise from 16 or 27 fathoms was quite immaterial.

I was just about to give the order to rise to the surface, when my glance fell on the gyro-compass, which with its slowly jerking black and white disc hangs usually so serenely in its case, which is lit up from the inside. . . .

I fell back in surprise. . . .

What on earth had come over it? The disc of the compass had gone quite mad and was turning round and round with short jerky movements. . . .

The affair began to grow distinctly uncomfortable. Considering that our gyro-compasses are about the most reliable of any in the whole world, and as at a depth of 27 fathoms in Chesapeake Bay the earth could hardly be revolving round us, there was only one conclusion to be drawn, and that a confoundedly unpleasant one. . . . We must be turning round and round in our hole, for what reason the devil only knew!

I immediately gave orders for the pumps to be started, with the result that they started rattling, but with a more clanking, empty noise, so to speak, than usual. . . . They did not help us in the least; we remained sticking in the mud, exactly as we were before.

This was the last straw, and I must confess our confidence began to waver somewhat. In the meantime we had sunk a little deeper according to the depth gauge, while, on the other hand, the rolling had ceased and we lay perfectly still.

Once more I gave energetic orders to rise immediately to the surface. The pumps started rattling and ran empty again. That was no good therefore.

The situation must be carefully thought out, otherwise we should be lying in the same place till morning.

After a lot of trouble the engineer, Klees, succeeded in getting the pumps into working order again.

With a deep humming sound they started pressing the water out of the tanks—they were working! As if transfixed our eyes sought the hand of the depth gauge. Hurrah! we were coming free, we were rising, the hand was pointing to 26 fathoms . . . could I trust my eyes . . . what the devil was that again? . . . the gauge suddenly pointed to 11 fathoms . . . then on again to 26 fathoms . . . and back to 11 once more. . . .

The affair was now growing critical. . . . We looked at each other, absolutely at the end of our resources, not knowing what was wrong with the boat or with ourselves, nor even at what depth we were . . . and now even the depth gauges had gone mad! . . .

In order to understand what this means, it must be clearly realised that in a submerged boat nothing can be known or seen, except by means of the hands of the depth gauge. If that once ceases to fulfil its functions correctly, then you are absolutely "at sea."

The situation had therefore grown very serious. Nevertheless, an iron calm reigned in the boat. We had the consolation that in the utmost emergency we could use our compressed air, which could not fail to bring us to the surface, even if the pumps failed us.

There was, however, no need to resort to this. Klees, who had been lost in thought, suddenly gripped hold of one of the valves—a hissing noise of compressed air, the depth gauge pointed wildly to 66 fathoms then sprang back to 26 again . . . then the coating of slime which had stopped up the spouts of the gauge was blown away by a little of the compressed air.

The mouths of the pumps were also cleared by means of the compressed air of all the mud and' slime which had worked in during our wild circular movements; then the pumps commenced humming in their usual tones, and the *Deutschland* rose obediently to the surface.

We had been, however, one hour and a half under water.

Captain Hinsch, in the *Timmins*, came alongside much relieved. He had been unable to understand the meaning of our long submersion and had grown extremely anxious.

We must apparently have got into some kind of pit, where the sand was being "ground" and where, owing to our circular movements, we dug our way gradually into the slime and mud. I then posted the *Timmins* at a distance of two miles away for an observation of a last important submersion test.

Our aim was, without advancing, to rise so that the periscope appeared above water, which was by no means an easy matter. It is naturally much easier to get up to a certain position by utilising the dynamical lift given by the diving rudders, but in doing this the periscope makes a little track of foam through the sea, which might under certain conditions prove treacherous.

We tried, therefore, to lift ourselves from a greater depth by oscillating up to a certain height and, by alternately emptying and filling the tanks at that depth, to reach a floating position in which only our periscope should appear just above the water, and that in a vertical direction.

The experiment succeeded. We were able to stretch out our periscope feelers so that the *Timmins*—who knew roughly our vicinity— did not notice us before our conning-tower appeared above the water.

I now felt certain that we were prepared for all possibilities and could risk breaking through unobserved. We continued therefore calmly on our way with *Timmins* and regulated our course so that we reached the exit between the capes just after darkness had set in.

CHAPTER 12

Running the Blockade

Night had set in as we approached the danger zone. In front of us sparkled the steady fire from Cape Henry, while astern Cape Charles threw out her lights at short intervals through the darkness. With these as our bearings we went on calmly to face the decision.

Suddenly two searchlights flashed out over the water to starboard. The accursed rays passed quick as lightning over the dark waves. I counted several seconds mechanically, then the full glare of the searchlight struck us in the eye. . . .

It was already too late to submerge, and the treacherous light held fast on to the *Deutschland*.

A rapid glance passed between the two of us in the tower, our features showed up distinctly in the beautiful free illumination. . . .

Then we saw that the rays of the searchlight, after they had made sure of us, rose twice high in the sky and suddenly disappeared. As our eyes grew accustomed to the darkness again, we discovered two black vessels to starboard which looked like fishing trawlers.

"The cursed gang!" murmured Krapohl, at my side; "now they have betrayed us!"

And he was right, unfortunately.

For over yonder on the coast a gigantic searchlight flashed high in the sky, obviously as a signal to the English cruisers waiting outside.

"Now was the moment," I thought.

"Make ready to submerge," my orders rang out.

"Ten fathoms down!"—at the same time we took a course to the south.

Half an hour later we rose to the surface again, as I wanted to take my bearings once more. Hardly had I taken a glance round, however, than we were obliged to avoid immediate danger by submerging

143

again. For close by, barely 200 yards off, an American armoured cruiser was bearing down on us.

She also had seen the remarkable flash signals, and was coming along to watch over the proceedings in the vicinity of American territorial waters. Although, according to the newspapers, the armoured cruiser was supposed to have been ordered into Chesapeake Bay for manoeuvres, I am of opinion that the American Government had ordered the ship to go out to the three-mile boundary line, in order to watch events in connection with our escape. I am also personally strongly convinced that the excellent tone in the officers' mess and among the crews of the American marine would not have allowed the men of the armoured cruiser, in the event of any violation of the territorial water zone, to restrict themselves merely to observation, but that they would have taken an energetic part in the proceedings.

That such a violation was not by any means beyond the realms of possibility, and that it was probably only prevented on that memorable night by the sudden appearance of the American armoured cruiser, is borne out by the following circumstance. Several days before our departure an English cruiser had passed Cape Henry under cover of mist and darkness and searched the whole of Chesapeake Bay in the most shameless manner, after which, without making her identity known, she disappeared again.

In the meantime we had quickly forced our boat heavily down by the head into the deeps, and did not rise to the surface again till the noise of the American's propeller had died away in the distance.

We knew that the most dangerous moment of our whole voyage was near at hand. We took a careful view of the situation once more, and made all the necessary preparations for our *Deutschland*.

Then we submerged again and went on, all our faculties strained to the uttermost, our nerves filled to overflowing with that cold excitement which inwardly, so to speak, causes one's hair to stand on end, while outwardly one is quite calm, gripped in that icily clear deliberation which only comes to those who are fully conscious that they are face to face with an unknown danger. . . .

We knew our way. It had been already brought to our knowledge that fishermen had been bribed to lay nets in stated positions outside the three-mile boundary line—nets in which we were to be caught fast, in which, moreover, devilish mines had been interwoven. . . . Or perhaps the nets might be merely attached to buoys, which we should drag along behind us, and thus betray our position. . . .

We were prepared for all contingencies, and had made everything ready to free ourselves from the nets if the worst should happen. But the worst did not happen.

It was a dark night. The lights from the two capes shone calmly, with friendly eyes on land, while a few miles farther out death lurked in every conceivable form.

But while the English ships travelled backwards and forwards, lighting up the waters with their searchlights and seeking us in every conceivable spot, they little knew that at times, close on their heels, a periscope proceeded on its leisurely way, and underneath this periscope—the U Deutschland.

At 12 p.m. that night, after hours of indescribable tension, the command rang out: "Rise to the surface!"

We were through.

Slowly the Deutschland rose through the water, the tanks were blown out and the oil engines started.

At full speed we rushed on out into the open freedom of the Atlantic, while behind us in the north-west, the English, with whole bundles of searchlights, sought the waters in vain.

They must have grown somewhat irritable towards the end!

CHAPTER 13

The Homeward Journey

Never had the *Deutschland* travelled so swiftly as in those early morning hours of the 3rd August. With marvellous speed she raced on, leaving two broad streaks of foam on either side.

The engines rumbled in perfect rhythm, the combustion was working without a flaw, and the exhaust showed not the slightest cloud, so that even Herr Kiszling was thoroughly contented, and in a moment of unconscious tenderness nearly stroked the shaft of his beloved engines. . . .

When the sun rose the coast had long disappeared from sight in the distance in a grey mist, and there was no vessel of any kind to be seen.

We remained on the surface and raced on like the very devil. How much we owed to our engines! On our arrival at Baltimore, after our long and difficult journey they had been still in perfect condition; no repairs were necessary, and we could have made the return journey immediately without their being overhauled. And yet the engines had been obliged to work under quite unknown conditions, under conditions which like that of the terrible temperature in the Gulf Stream had made the very highest and most unforeseen demands on every part of the machinery.

It can be easily understood that hitherto there had been no opportunity of testing the working capabilities of oil motors in an outside temperature of 127 degrees Fahrenheit. Such a contingency could never have been foreseen in the construction of our type of boat, and the fact that our motors never struck, that not the least hitch arose, proves the excellence of the construction and the perfect workmanship of the dockyard.

Thus we continued on our way, and only too soon found ourselves in the damp heated atmosphere and heavy air of the Gulf Stream, with all its beautiful phenomena and peculiarities, its electrically laden air and stormy sea. With closed hatches and heat in the boat we faced it once more. And the Stream would not even help to push us along on our course, as we had hoped.

All hardships were, however, borne with light hearts this time. We had left the danger zone behind us, and were homeward bound. Moreover, the sea had become calmer the nearer we approached the area of the Gulf Stream.

On the evening of the second day it had become possible to open all the deck hatches again. Hardly had we begun to rejoice that the fresh air would now make conditions below deck bearable once more, when suddenly the order came, "Close hatches!" "Submerge!"

A steamer had appeared and was rapidly approaching so directly in our course that we could not possibly have avoided her above water.

When we rose to the surface again an hour later night had set in, and with it appeared a most marvellous natural phenomenon of sea phosphorescence of unearthly splendour.

We had submerged in a calm dark sea; we now arose to an ocean of flame. A sea phosphorescence had set in of an intensity and glow such as I had never before experienced, and which is probably only to be found on the borders of the Gulf Stream.

During our rise, and when we were at about 2 fathoms below the surface, it seemed as if we were working upwards through a glowing realm of sparkling transparency. Shortly before the conning-tower arose above water I glanced round astern, and saw the entire hull of the boat, with the stern like a dark mass pushing its way through the glowing element. A fiery whirlpool radiated from the propeller, and every movement of the boat aroused the wildest phosphorescence— intensive flames, sprays of sparks, and fiery streaks in the surrounding waters.

Above, a fresh breeze had set in and whipped the seething waters into glowing balls, while showers of sparkling foam covered the entire deck. As far as the eye could reach the surface of the sea was one pale glowing mass, through which our boat ploughed its way in furrows of fire.

We stood transfixed as the phenomenon increased in intensity with the sea and wind.

All the men off duty came up and stared out at this enchanting spectacle, little heeding the seas which swept over the deck, soaking many of them through to the skin.

"It looks like fire, don't it? But blowed if it don't put yer pipe out," remarked our giant boatswain. A spurt had just extinguished his pipe for the third time, and he reluctantly decided to store the beloved stump carefully in his pocket.

But the "fire" grew wetter and wetter, and within half an hour the officers on duty and lookout stood once more alone up in the conning-tower.

When we got out of the Gulf Stream we had several days of stiff north-westerly winds and high seas, until, on the August, we ran into fine weather again.

On one of the following evenings the first officer on duty, Krapohl, was standing with Humke in the conning-tower scanning the horizon without ceasing, through the glasses, at a point where the pale sky seemed to merge into the sea without any observable boundary line.

"Light ahead," announced Humke suddenly.

"If you mean that star, I've noticed it already," the officer replied, calmly lowering his glasses.

"Wal, I dunno, but that there ain't no star, Herr Krapohl," the sailor replied, unabashed.

The two called out to me, and I came expectantly out of the tower, took the glasses and then laughed.

"Humke, you're on the wrong track!" for I noticed high up above the horizon a faint white light which stood too high, judging by its strength, to be a ship's light.

The boatswain stolidly maintained his opinion, however.

"Cap'n, that there ain't no star."

I handed him the glasses which he, however, put aside at once, remarking:

"Ye can't see nothink properly with them things."

He shut his eyes tightly, then took another sharp look and said in decided tones:

"That ain't no star; that be a light!"

We stared before us with increased sharpness till I was able at last to make out through the glasses a red glow which now became visible to the right of the white light. Now we knew that a steamer was approaching us.

At first I held her to be a small vessel, particularly as, to begin with, the height of the two lights differed but slightly—the red port light of the steamer was not much below the white light.

But soon I was surprised to observe how noticeably the red light moved, that is to say, how quickly the space between the two lights appeared to increase.

From this there was only one possible conclusion to be drawn, and that was that the vessel was approaching with extraordinary rapidity.

While I was considering this, and picturing it to myself as a swiftly travelling destroyer, I discovered at a fair distance behind the two lights something that looked like a white moving ray, or like a faintly illuminated wave.

We could not make out what this meant till I decided that this wave must belong to the lights themselves, as they moved together and kept pace with each other. And a few minutes later there appeared tremblingly on the strong lens of the glasses the faint outline of a mighty steamer, which with elaborate superstructure was approaching in the dark night. The white ray of light was her stern water, which owing to the colossal length of the ship was only visible at a considerable distance from her side lights.

For some minutes longer we continued to stare, then we discovered four towering funnels, and were soon convinced that we had a big Cunard liner in front of us which was racing up in semi-darkness, only showing her headlights.

It really was a ghostly apparition, to observe how the mighty darkened ship raced on through the night. There is not much need to be romantically inclined in order to picture this, meeting with the *Flying Dutchman*, while Humke expressed his feelings in the words: "Lor', ain't she just a beauty, lads!"

"Full speed ahead!" and with "helm hard a-starboard" we slipped away from the course of the mighty Cunarder. All the men of the watch off duty meanwhile had come up to get a view of her from the deck and hatches.

In spite of a sharp look-out nothing appeared in sight during the next few days. The weather keeping fine our homeward journey—even more than when we were outward-bound—assumed the character of a peaceful, uneventful business voyage.

It was now that we first began fully to appreciate the convenient and practical inner fittings of the whole boat, and particularly our cabins and cosy little mess-room. Often as we sat round the table at mess while the gramophones played gaily, we thought with gratitude of those who had not only invented the seaworthy shape of our boat, but had fitted her interior up so that a life of comparative comfort and ease was possible even under the sea.

When on these occasions our gallant Stucke, with his blonde white hair, his honest face full of earnest gravity, and his habitually surprised expression placed a bottle of good red Californian wine in front of us, as we lay comfortably "somewhere" at the bottom of the sea, while overhead, at a height of X fathoms, a hearty wind was blowing, it needed little imagination to picture oneself as a second Captain Nemo, who with his highly modern Nautilus could probe the depths, and snap his fingers at the injustice and tyranny of a certain people—provided, that is to say, one had read Jules Verne.

For I must here confess, what I had hitherto carefully concealed from everyone, that it was only as captain of a submarine trader on my return journey from America that I was enabled to make good a very sad deficiency in my education. The chance I had wasted in my youth I now came across at the age of forty-nine in the steel body of the *U Deutschland*, of making myself acquainted with Jules Verne's *Twenty Thousand Leagues under the Sea*.

The book had been sent me while I was at Baltimore through the kindness of an American friend. It is a book—how shall I describe it?—of incitement and emulation. I read it with the greatest interest.

★★★★★★

The rest of our return journey is soon told. We travelled on smoothly and peacefully homewards, avoiding a few distant steamers above water—in which little game we had gradually become extremely well practised—and meeting on the whole with good weather, some mist, and much smooth sea.

One afternoon I was sitting working at the writing-table in my cabin, when suddenly I heard from the control-room close by the order "20 to starboard" repeated. Immediately after came "10 to port," whereupon, without waiting to hear any more, I hurried on deck.

There a strange sight awaited me. All around, as far as the eye could reach, the sea was covered with a mass of dark, floating oil casks through which we had to steer our way.

At first I took the black, weird-looking objects, which danced up and down on the waves before us, for a minefield, until the characteristic shape of the sharp angular casks, or so-called barrels, and their contents which had spread partly over the water, testified to their harmlessness. Nevertheless we had to steer carefully through this strange plantation, as the area was too wide a one to avoid without going considerably out of our course. We estimated the number of casks that were visible to us as at least a thousand.

"Fine practice," remarked Krapohl, "for the elegance with which we shall twist through the English minefields later on. I think we might risk the return through the English Channel."

We went on, therefore, at half-speed to port—starboard—port, for over an hour. Scattered parts of vessels were to be seen on the water, possibly the results of wrecks or mines.

We must by this time have gradually come within the sphere of the English lookout ships. The watch was doubled, everyone standing at their submerging stations.

From time to time we noticed vessels whose attention we avoided by submerging or altering our course. One warship, apparently a small English cruiser, we allowed no possibility of seeing us by immediately diving. When, after an hour's under-sea journey, we again rose slowly to the surface, we saw from a depth of 6½ fathoms, through the periscope, another English ship, and went down again to 11 fathoms, and this was repeated three times in succession.

At noon we rose at last for good, emptied the tanks, and then travelled at top speed over the water.

Favoured by the fine weather we approached our goal with considerable rapidity; and on August —— at eight o'clock in the evening, we saw a circle of white lights all round the horizon.

Our natural fear was, of course, that we were surrounded; if we turned to starboard we saw those accursed lights, to port—there they were too.

Finally our excellent Zeiss glasses removed our fears that at the last moment with the homeland already in sight we had fallen into a trap. The twilight was still clear enough to allow us to see and recognize from the construction of the uncanny-looking ships that only some harmless Dutch fishing boats lay before us.

CHAPTER 14

The Arrival

Favourable winds astern helped us on towards home. On August —— at six o'clock in the morning, our alarm was raised once more. In the far distance something appeared on the water which looked like the sail of a boat, though certainly of a very strange appearance. As it approached nearer the sail turned out to be the conning-tower of a U-Boat, which, with her deck still dripping, was going on her way.

Although we were at first inclined to take careful and instructive observations of the strange object in the distance, in order to judge how we ourselves showed up at a distance of three knots, the best course in our case appeared to be to find out as quickly as possible if she were an English or a German submarine.

We preferred, however, in any case to make ourselves as unnoticeable as possible, and in the last emergency to submerge.

We had already flooded up to tank 3, already the sea broke over the deck and struck against the conning-tower, and even the latter was cutting half-way down through the green waters—when suddenly a well-known flag signal rose yonder, which gave us the certainty that it was a German U-Boat in front of us.

We answered immediately, and gave the command directly after:

"Empty the ballast tanks!"

Never had I given orders with such a cheerful heart on the *Deutschland* before, and never was it more cheerfully carried out than when I called down to the control-room:

"Hurrah! the first German U-Boat in sight!"

What did it matter that we were standing on the tower and the barely risen deck in oil and sea water with a shower-bath playing over us? . . . There, over the green North Sea, came the first greeting of Germany, the mighty Fatherland, towards us! At full speed we rushed on, everyone on deck, and before long the two boats lay within calling distance of each other.

The first ear-splitting hurrah was flung across to us, and answered in like manner.

Then greetings and news were exchanged, and our ways parted again ... ours towards home, the U-X to her work.

The day drew in and night fell once more. So we travelled homewards, no light on deck, no light in the tower—like a dark shadow.

When the sun rose, however, on the following morning, we saw before us in the distance a characteristic silhouette, breaking through the veil of mist in a rosy light. An island, a bulwark in the North Sea—Heligoland lay before us.

Soon life began to awaken on the waters around us. Torpedo-boats shot up, patrol boats hurried along, flag signals fluttered in the air, wireless signals rattled out their greetings, and shouting and hand-wavings commenced, and then the iron ring of the German Fleet, which keeps safe watch over yonder, closed round our little *Deutschland*, and under their protection we steered on past Heligoland towards the home haven.

But as we approached the well-known waters, even before the low homelike sandy coast came in sight, a wonderful spectacle fell to our lot, the strangest of greetings carried out with the utmost skill.

From the land two huge birds seemed to rise into the air—two seaplanes which approached at full speed and then sank like gigantic water-fowls on the gently moving surface of the sea.

They shot down with their floats just brushing the surface of the water, till within a stone's throw of the *Deutschland*, made a lightning turn, crashing by us, approached again and sprang literally over our heads, racing low down over the conning-tower, with cheers and waving of caps. . .

This was our reception from the latest weapon of the German Navy.

One should not make comparisons. But as we once more approached the German coast, surrounded and protected by the German Marine, I suddenly found myself comparing this with our arrival in America.

No one could have been received with more hearty enthusiasm than we had been by the Americans. A free, untroubled people, they rejoiced in a bold deed, and openly declared their sympathy for a new and unheard of enterprise, which it had required men to fulfil.

But here we were more than bold and interesting adventurers. Here our own people received us again as helpmates in their mighty struggle. Here the delightful spectacle of her power under the sea, on the sea, and in the air was presented to us.

This was for me the real meaning of the glorious greeting of our airmen. This was what I felt as the lookout boats accompanied us safely as far as the outer Weser, where we cast anchor before the Hohenweg lighthouse, for the first time after many a long day.

CHAPTER 15

The Reception of the "Deutschland"
by the German People

From the outskirts of Heligoland as far as the outer Weser we had been received by the Navy. On the voyage up the Weser and at Bremen the whole nation received us.

On the afternoon of the 23rd August the *Deutschland* had struck anchor at the mouth of the Weser. The news had been spread by telegraph throughout the whole country—this longed-for news, which awakened unbounded rejoicings.

We learnt to our surprise and proud delight that the arrival of the *Deutschland* was to inaugurate a festive holiday for the whole German people, that such a reception awaited our little boat on the banks of the Weser as surely never fell to the lot of any "lucky ship" before. Our journey up the Weser assumed the nature of a triumphal procession. Behind the hundreds of thousands who had come to meet us and stood cheering on the banks, stood invisible the millions of German people inspired with the same feeling.

This was expressed to us everywhere in overwhelming rejoicings from old and young, high and low, from the German *Kaiser* down to the merest dock worker and the small ragged urchin who, full of enthusiasm, waved his flag and shouted in the streets of Bremen.

On the 25th August, early in the morning, the *Deutschland* commenced her triumphal trip up the Weser. It poured in torrents, but nothing could quench the public rejoicings as we moved along accompanied by the blockaded steamers, our masts and conning-tower decorated with garlands of roses.

Low hung the dark clouds in the heavens, and the rain pelted down on the thousands who stood on the dykes or who had come

155

to meet us on steamers, barges, launches, and rowing boats. Deafening cheers arose from the town, and the clashing of bells mingled with the joyful acclamations, while above it all rose the song of "*Deutschland, Deutschland über alles*," which on that very day was celebrating its seventy-fifth birthday.

In Nordenham, Brake, Blumeuthal, flags salute, guns thunder out, factory and steamer whistles send their piercing greetings; shouts of welcome and good wishes ring out from the North German Lloyd steamers, to which we respond by waving back.

Vegesack is passed, where work on the Vulcan Docks has ceased, the dockers standing in hundreds on the quay. Their wild cheers accompany the *Deutschland* on her triumphal way. The inhabitants of Vegesack are all assembled at the landing-place and on the banks behind.

Again music and singing, the roar of guns and storms of rejoicing! Thicker and thicker grow the crowds as the ship nears her home haven.

Shortly before twelve we reached Lankenau, whose dyke had been chosen as an observation point by the whole of Bremen, it appeared. Elbow to elbow the people stood waving with hats, umbrellas, handkerchiefs, hands. . . .

At noon punctually the *Deutschland* sailed into the open harbour, and placed her invited guests, 'mid sounds of "*Deutschland über alles*," on the highly decorated pontoon, on which the Grand Duke of Oldenburg, the representatives of the Bremen Senate and *burghership*, the civilian and military authorities, the marine, the shipping officials, etc., and among them Count Zeppelin, were all assembled to receive us.

As soon as the ship was moored I called the men up to take their positions on deck. Dr. Lohmann then addressed us in the following speech:

Your Royal Highness, Your Magnificencies, Your Excellencies, My very honoured friends,—At this historical moment of the happy return of the first submarine merchant-trader of the world, after a voyage of 8,500 knots, I here welcome our *Deutschland* and her gallant crew, not only in the name of our shipping officials, but of the whole German people, back to the harbour of their homeland. Quietly and only known to an initiated few, they left the Weser, passed through and under the English Fleet, to arrive on the 10th July at Baltimore with a valuable cargo of dyes. Their arrival was a surprise to the whole world. Even navigation experts shortly before this event had declared it to be an impossible undertaking.

It is with particular pleasure that I am able to state that all true Americans who are not demoralised by a degrading Mammon service to England—men with the freedom-loving instincts of a Washington and a Franklin, greeted the arrival of the *Deutschland* in America with warmest satisfaction. It is the pride of our shipping officials that we have been able to send dyes to America under the German flag in the middle of this war, while America herself cannot even get her post from Europe unmolested, to say nothing of the many other violations of the rights of humanity by sea and land on the part of our enemy, in connection with the neutrals, and particularly the small states.

To accomplish this has been the work of the crew of the *Deutschland*. Though they started off without any previous announcement, their departure from Baltimore was made publicly known beforehand. 'It resembled a triumphal procession,' wrote Havas, 'and a symbol of freedom.' I myself should like to compare the deed with our German view of the 'Rights of the Peoples on the free Ocean.' The enemy were not able to prevent their departure from Chesapeake Bay, and a blockaded North Sea did not exist for them on their return voyage, as will be proved by the many million *marks*' worth of goods which have today been brought from America, and which lie at this moment before our eyes.

They have performed a task of seamanship that is worthy of our Hanseatic forefathers. Everywhere throughout German lands, and among our faithful allies, but particularly among our brothers in the trenches and in the fleet, their return voyage has been followed with deepest sympathy. With strongest confidence in their judgment, energy, and sense of duty, we members of the shipping world have looked forward to their return. After their long and strenuous weeks in the narrow confines of a ship, face to face with unscrupulous enemies, I welcome them heartily back to the Homeland. In the midst of this murderous war I convey to them the thanks of our German people for their peaceful deed. And I should like to express these thanks by calling for three cheers for the *Deutschland*, her commander, Captain König, her officers and crew. Hurrah! Hurrah! Hurrah!

I answered with a brief toast to the Senate and *burghership* of the free Hansa city Bremen. We then boarded the pontoon, where each one of us was saluted and drawn into conversation by the Grand Duke of Oldenburg and the other gentlemen present.

After completing a distance of 8,450 knots, from which only about 190 under water must be deducted, the first submarine merchant-trader had reached home. The *Deutschland's* first voyage to America was completed.

★★★★★★

On the evening of this memorable day a big dinner was given at the Town Hall by the Municipality of the borough of Bremen, to celebrate the homecoming of the *Deutschland*. The speeches that were delivered on this occasion give a short outline of the circumstances which led to the building of the *Deutschland*, and for this reason they shall be repeated here.

Dr. Barkhausen, the mayor, had received his guests with words of hearty welcome, and informed them of the Municipality's decision to have a special medal struck in memory of the day, and had then toasted the German shipping officials, and the crew of the submarine merchant-trader *Deutschland*.

In the name of the Shipping Federation, their chief representative, Dr. A. Lohmann, replied in the following words:

Your Magnificencies, Your Excellencies, my most honoured gentlemen,—In the name of the commander of the *Deutschland*, Captain König, and of his officers and crew, I wish to express to the Municipality their most heartfelt thanks, as also that of the Shipping Federation, for the great honour granted by the Municipality to the crew of the *Deutschland* in allowing a medal to be struck in commemoration of this peaceful commercial deed in the midst of war.

I wish to thank your Excellencies for the words in which you have graciously acknowledged the work of my colleagues and myself. Since the outbreak of war I have gladly and willingly devoted my efforts towards the welfare of the State. The conviction that our splendid people, in spite of the superior force of the enemy, are not to be crushed in this defensive war for their individuality and freedom, that the intellectual power and forethought which inspire our entire people, their thorough training since the wars of liberation, and the inborn sense of duty which has come down to every German in flesh and blood, are not to be overcome, this conviction has accompanied me throughout all my efforts, and everywhere I have met faithful colleagues who were of the same opinion.

I should like therefore at this point to express my heartfelt thanks to all my fellow-workers, and in particular to Herr Direktor Stapelfeldts, and my colleagues on the Board, Herr General-Direktor Heineken, and Herr Hermann, Councillor of Commerce. The German Ocean Shipping Federation was formed, as your Excellencies have already stated, in all secrecy, and their task consisted in forwarding goods of the utmost possible value.

It meant, moreover, purchasing the raw materials on the other side, their careful warehousing, the placing of the *Deutschland* in a safe position, and protecting her from all attacks. This was carried out to perfection by the North German Lloyd agents, Herr Paul Hilken and his father, Herr Hilken, Senior, as well as by Captain Hinsch and his co-operators. The share which Captain König and his officers and crew took in the enterprise has already been brought into prominence by your Excellencies. For my part and on behalf of the shipping directors, I should like here once more to tender our fellow-workers on the *Deutschland* our very hearty thanks.

It will interest the gentlemen present to hear something of the history of the German Ocean Shipping Federation and of the *Deutschland*, the *Bremen*, and her as yet unnamed sister-ships.

"When in September, 1915, it became evident that, in spite of all the successes of the Central Powers, the war would continue for many months yet, it was obvious that Germany's demand for rubber and metals was of burning necessity.

I therefore took the shipbuilding authorities in Bremen into my confidence, after I had held counsel with one of the most prominent ship-building experts. The *Weser* declared itself ready to draw up and carry out the plans for a submarine boat of about 500 tons carrying power. On the 3rd October I came into possession of the completed plans of this boat. The period of construction unfortunately ran into eleven months, the delivery being therefore completed about September 1st, 1916, for the docks were first obliged to have the motors built. It was obvious that we must make an effort another time if possible to reach our object more quickly. Almost at the same time that the practical evolution of a submarine merchant-man was under our consideration, the Germania Dock at Kiel had, unknown to us, handed over at the beginning of October to their chief house, Friedrich Krupp and Sons, plans for the construction of a U-Boat of about 700 tons carrying capacity.

The Germania Docks were prepared, in the short space of six months, to deliver the first boat, the *Deutschland*, as early as April.

Both plans, those of the Germania Docks as well as my own, showed that the project was possible to carry out, and I should like to compare this community of ideas with a happy marriage, where husband and wife are in perfect harmony with each other—the dockyard, as the mother who brings the child into the world and gives it to the father—the shipowners and commerce—to place it in the world. The soul and mind of the child were incorporated in our Captain, our officers and crew, who have performed the glorious task of taking the *Deutschland* to America and back.

On the 15th October we had come to an agreement, and the construction of two boats was taken over by the Germania Docks from the Syndicate. The formal part of the establishment of the German Ocean Shipping Federation was delayed somewhat. Its establishment took place on the 8th November, and the boats which had in the meantime been ordered by our Syndicate were already under construction as far as their framework. The *Deutschland* was delivered over to us at the beginning of April.

It was a wonderful masterpiece of the Germania Docks, and, as is usual with all the work of Messrs. Friedrich Krupp and Sons, it was perfectly carried out. Before we sent our *Deutschland* to America, we made trial trips with her for over two months. The execution of the work proved to have been carried out perfectly in every respect. Captain König was able to announce from America that after a voyage of over 4,000 knots ship and machinery were in perfect working order; his report on arriving here in Bremen harbour was just the same. It is a masterpiece of German technique, and the name of Messrs. Krupp and Sons appears in shining colours once again.

From the creation of our artillery, from the 42's down to the smallest specimen of ship guns that began successfully to break the chain of the British Fleet in the Skagerrack and prepare the way for free trade among the nations, to the production of arms and war material of every description—the German people now owe their thanks for this perfect piece of construction to the ingenious leaders and directors of the greatest works in the world. Without Krupp, our enemies would not now, after two years of war, be standing everywhere on the other side of their boundary lines.

The intelligent co-operation of mind and body, the employment of all the newest scientific discoveries, added to the true German sense of duty, these are the qualities that have made Krupp and Sons famous. Today, on the return of the *Deutschland*, we are face to face with another wonderful production of shipbuilding technique on the part of the firm of Krupp, and for this also the German people owe their thanks to them. I should like to ask you all, gentlemen, to give expression to these thanks by joining with me in three hearty cheers.

The firm of Friedrich Krupp and Sons, Germania Docks. Hurrah! Hurrah! Hurrah!

After the next course, Herr Zetzmann, the Director of the Germania Docks at Kiel, proceeded as follows:

Your Magnificencies, Your Excellencies, Most honoured gentlemen,—To my lot has fallen the honour of expressing in the name of the firm of Friedrich Krupp and Sons and of the Germania Docks, our heartiest thanks for the invitation that has been extended us today by the Municipality, and I also take the liberty of extending my thanks to the distinguished guests of the Corporation assembled here.

. . . Herr Lohmann has made some interesting communications in his speech with regard to the history of the origin of the German Ocean Shipping Federation, and I should like to add a few words about the workshop from which the *Deutschland* and *Bremen* sprang. We had been forced to admit for some time past, that owing to the continued duration of the war the need of certain building materials was becoming increasingly-urgent.

From the conversational remarks 'it might be possible,' and 'we really ought to,' arose the decision to consider seriously the possibility of a new kind of trading vessel.

The decision was no easy one, not merely because we feared the difficulty of construction, but because we hardly dared to place a fresh load on our building yards, which were already heavily overburdened with war orders. But necessity teaches how to beg,—and also how to construct! We next tried to work on the foundations of our war boats, in the hope that by this means we should lessen the constructional work. We found, however, that on these lines reliable tonnage capacity and carefully measured space were not to be attained.

Our leading constructors advised me, therefore, to go radically to work, and not to try and make a trader out of a warship, but to create a new type of trading boat altogether. The shape of this was to be made full and rounded, and exact calculations gave us a better tonnage, much to our surprise and pleasure, than we had anticipated at the commencement of our project. With wild enthusiasm our constructors completed their plans, and soon we stood face to. face with a picture whose transformation into reality would express our every wish.

. . . Herr Krupp von Bohlen and the Directors seized on our proposal with the greatest energy . . . and declared that a boat of this type must most certainly be produced, and in the shortest possible space of time, that moreover the Germania Docks would begin directly on the construction of the boat on their own responsibility.

. . . Everything went like clockwork. . . . There remains only one thing more for me to say. That we succeeded in completing the first boat in so short a space of time is due in a great measure to our principal firm and to our contractors, who delivered all our building materials and necessary fittings in spite of the other great demands that were made upon them, with astonishing rapidity.

I wish particularly to express my appreciation that all the dealings with the German Ocean Shipping Federation, and later with the staff of the boat, were completed in the most friendly of spirits. Both Shipping Federation and command staff have met all our proposals with the greatest confidence.

It is owing to this intelligent and broad-minded preference that the rapidity of the construction was made possible, and that the trial voyages went so smoothly. With the greatest confidence, therefore, we saw the ship undertake her first voyage.

Our confidence has brilliantly justified itself. Our most ardent wishes with which we followed this product of our dockyard have been fully realised.

We wish the Shipping Federation further brilliant successes of this kind, the *Deutschland* and her sister ships many equally happy voyages, for the welfare of our beloved Fatherland, and for the glory of our revered Hansa city, Bremen.

Today's celebration will be for all who have taken part in it a remembrance that they will carry to the end of their lives, and the celebration has been brought to a close in the most approved fashion by the dinner given in the new Town Hall by the Municipality. When this new part of the Town Hall has grown as time-worn as the old, perhaps tales will be told of how the successful ocean voyage of the first submarine merchant-trader in the world was celebrated here.

Together with our thanks for the splendid feast, I should like to join my good wishes for Bremen, and I ask the honourable gentlemen present to join in the toast: 'Long life and prosperity to the Municipal Corporation of the free Hansa City of Bremen and to the town of Bremen. Hurrah! Hurrah! Hurrah!'

The Adventures of the U-202

Baron Spiegel
Von Und Zu Peckelsheim

Contents

Preface

I was sitting on the conning tower smoking a cigarette. Then the splash of a wave soaked it. I tried to draw another puff. It tasted loathsome and frizzled. Then I became angry and threw it away.

I can see my reader's surprised expression. You had expected to read a serious U-boat story and now such a ridiculous beginning! But I know what I am doing. If I had once thrown myself into the complicated U-boat system and used a bunch of technical terms, this story would be shorter and more quickly read through, but you would not have understood half of it.

Seriousness will come, bitter and pitiable seriousness. In fact, everything is serious which is connected with the life on board a submarine and none of it is funny; although in fact it is the hundred small inconveniences and peculiar conditions on a U-boat which make life on it remarkably characteristic. And in order to bring to the public a closer knowledge concerning the peculiar life on board a U-boat I am writing this story. Good—therefore my log-book! Yes, why should I not make use of it?

To this I also wish to add that I not only used my own log-book but also at many places had use of other U-boats' logs in order to present one or another episode which is worth the while relating. Thus, for example, the story of the many fishing-smacks, which are spoken of in the chapter called "Rich Spoils," is borrowed, but the happenings in the witch kettle, the adventure with the English bulldog, and also most of the other chapters are my own feathers with which I have adorned this little story. This is the only liberal right of an author which I permit myself. The style of the story from a log-book is simple and convenient, and one buys so willingly such stories. See there two valid reasons for making use of it.

The Author.

1

Our First Success

At the hunting grounds North Sea, April 12, 19— Course: northwest.
Wind: southwest, strength 3-4. Sea: strength 3. View: good. Both machines
in high speed.

We were very comfortable in the conning tower because the weather was fine and the sun burned with its heat our field-gray skin jackets.

"Soon we will have summer," I said to the officer on guard, Lieutenant Petersen, who was sitting with me on the conning tower's platform. I felt entirely too hot in my thick underwear.

Petersen, who, like me, was sitting with his legs dangling in the open hatch on whose edge we had placed ourselves, put his hand on the deck and loosened the thick, camel's wool scarf, twice wrapped around his neck, as if suddenly he realized it was too hot for him, too.

"I think I'll soon discharge this one from service," said Petersen, and pulled at the faithful winter friend as if he wished to strip it off.

"Don't be too hasty, my dear lieutenant," I replied laughing. "Just wait until tonight, and then I am sure that you will repent and take your faithful friend back into the service."

"Are we going to keep above the water tonight, *Herr* Captain-Lieutenant, or are we to submerge?" he asked me.

"It depends on what comes up," I answered. "It rests as usual with the weather."

Thus we were talking and smoking on the conning tower while our eyes scanned the horizon and kept a sharp lookout all around us.

On the little platform, which in a sharp angle triangle unites itself from behind with the tower, the subordinate officer corporal was on guard, and with a skin cloth was cleaning the lenses on his double spy-

171

glass, which were wet.

"Did you also get a dousing, Krappohl?" I asked. "Then you didn't look out, either. That rascal soaked my cigarette just as he did the lenses on your spy-glass. That's the dickens of a trick."

With the word "rascal" I meant the splashing wave, which, while the sea was in a perfect calm, without any reason climbed up to us on the tower. If there had been a storm it would have been nothing to mention. Then we often did not have a dry thread on our bodies. But such a shameless scoundrel, which in the midst of the most beautiful weather suddenly throws himself over a person, is something to make one angry.

We made good speed. The water, which was thrown aside by the bow, passed by us in two wide white formed streaks. The motor rattled and rumbled, and the ventilation machine in the so-called "*Centrale*" right under our feet made a monotonous buzzing. Through the only opening where the air could pass out, the open tower hatch, all kinds of odours flowed one after another from the lower regions right by our noses. First we smelled smear-oil. Then the fragrance of oranges (we had with us a large shipment, which we had received as a gift of love), and now—ah! Now it was coffee, a strong aromatic coffee odor.

Lieutenant Petersen moved back and forth unrestingly on the "swimwest," with which he had tried to make it a little more comfortable for himself on the hard sitting place, bent deeper and deeper down into the hatch inhaling with greed the odour from below, and said, as he in pleasant anticipation began to rub his hands together:

"Now we'll have coffee, *Herr* Captain-Lieutenant!"

I had just with a great deal of trouble pulled out a cigarette-case from the inside pocket of my skin jacket and was groping in my other pockets for matches, when a hand (the gloves number 9½) with outstretched forefinger reached towards me from behind and the subordinate officer's excited voice announced:

"A cloud of smoke four points port."

As quickly as lightning the spy-glass was placed to the eye. "Where? Oh, yes, there. I can see it!"

"As yet, only smoke can be seen. Isn't it so?"

In what a suspense we were now. Leaning forward, and with the glasses pressed to the eye, we gazed on the little, distant, cloud of smoke. It curled, then bent with the wind and slowly dissolved in a long, thin veil-like streak. Nothing but smoke could be seen, a sign that the air was clear, and one could see all the way to the extreme horizon.

What kind of a ship could it be, which the curved form of the earth still concealed from our view? Was it a harmless freighter, a proud passenger steamer, an auxiliary cruiser, or maybe an armored cruiser jammed with cannon?

It was with a feeling, wavering between hope and fear, that these thoughts occupied my mind—fear, not for the enemy, because we were anxious to meet him—but fear that a disappointment would fall on us, if the ship proved to be a neutral steamer when it came closer. Seven times we had during three days experienced such disappointment, seven times we had met neutral ships without contraband on board, and had been compelled to let them continue on their way.

The distance between us and the steamer had not diminished, so that its masts and a funnel arose above the horizon, two narrow, somewhat slanting lines, between which there was a thicker dark spot. A common freighter, therefore. This we saw at the first glance. I changed our course northwardly in order to head off the course of the steamer which was going in an easterly direction. With the highest speed the machine could make we raced to meet them and the bridge and part of the hull could already be seen.

"To the diving stations! Artillery alarm. Cannon service on deck! First torpedo tube ready for fire!"

With loud voice I called down these commands into the boat.

There was a stir in the passages below like when a stone is thrown into the midst of a swarm of bees. From below it arose, and the men who were to serve at the cannons crowded on the narrow precipitous ladder, swung themselves through the tower hatch and leaped on the deck. Now, first, just once, a deep breath, so that the lungs can draw the refreshing sea air, and then with their sleeves turned up and flashing eyes to the guns.

"Can you see any neutral signs, Petersen?"

"No, *Herr* Captain-Lieutenant. The entire hull is black. It's an Englishman."

"The flag of war to the mast! The usual signals ready!" I called down into the tower.

Immediately our flag of war floated from the top of the mast behind the tower. It told the men over there: "Here am I, a German submarine U-boat. Now for it, you proud Britisher! Now it will be seen who rules the sea."

173

We had gradually drawn closer to a distance of about six thousand metres. At last an enemy! After so many neutral steamers. At last an enemy! An intense joy thrilled us, a joy which only can be compared with the hunter's when he sees at last the longed-for prey coming within range, after long and fruitless efforts. We had travelled many hundred sea miles. We had endured storm, cold, and at times had been drenched to the skin, and there, only two points port, our first success was waving towards us!

By this time we must have been discovered by the steamer. Now our flag of war must have been recognized. A ghastly horror must have seized the captain on the bridge: The U-boat terror! The U-boat pest!

But the captain on the steamer did not give in so easily. He tried to save himself by flight. Suddenly we saw how the steamer belched forth thicker and darker clouds of smoke and in a sharp curve turned port. Its propeller water, which hitherto could hardly be seen, was whipped to a white foam, and let us know the machines had been put into the highest possible speed. But it was of no use. No matter how much the captain was shouting and how much the machinist drove his sweating and naked fire crew to even more than human endeavors, so that the coal flew about and the boilers were red, everything was useless. We closed in on him with a horrible certainty nearer and nearer.

For some time I had been standing high up on the tower with a spy-glass before my eyes and did not lose one of the steamer's motions. Now it seemed to me the right moment had come to energetically command the steamer to stop.

"A shot above the steamer! Fire!"

The granite landed two hundred metres in front of the steamer. We waited a few minutes, but when the shot did not cause any change I gave the right distance to the gunners and shouted the command to aim at the steamer. The second shot hit and a thick, black and yellow cloud from the explosion shot into the air. The third shot tore a piece off the funnel, the fourth hit the bridge, and before the fifth had left the mouth of the gun the signal flew up, "I have stopped."

Ah! Old friend, you had come to it, anyhow!

An old sea-rule says: "Carefulness is the best seamanship." Regarding all the tricks and subterfuges which the hostile merchant-marine has used against us, I did not consider it advisable to advance nearer the steamer at once. I therefore also stopped our machines and signalled: "Leave the ship immediately!"

The signal was unnecessary. The English captain had himself given the command to the crew to take to the boats after he, frothing with anger, had comprehended the impossibility to flee. Snorting with wrath, he shortly afterwards came alongside our boat, and handed me at my request the ship's papers and asked me to tow the three boats to the neighbourhood of the coast. I promised this and said some simple words to him in regard to his bad luck and concerning the grim necessity of the war—which he dismissed with an angry shrug of his shoulders. I certainly could understand the man's bad spirit.

I then went forward and torpedoed the steamer, which sank, stern foremost, with a gurgling sound into the deep.

At the same time four thousand tons of rice were lost to the English market.

We had met with success and this put us into the highest spirits. Come whatever wants to come, our voyage had not been entirely useless.

When I stepped down into the boat for a moment and passed through the narrow crew-room to my own little cabin, I saw to right and left joyful faces, and all eyes were smiling towards me as if they wished to say: "Congratulations!" The steamer's sinking was the subject of discussion. Those who had witnessed the incident had to describe all the circumstances in smallest detail; where the torpedo had struck, how high the water-pillar had risen, and what afterwards happened to the steamer, how the people on the boat looked, and the like. Everything had to be explained.

When I went back someone said: "Tomorrow it will be in the papers." These words whirled around in my head for some time. Yes, tomorrow there would be in all the German newspapers under the column: "Ships sunk" or "Sacrifices to the U-boat war," that once more we had retaliated on our most hated enemy, that his inhuman attempt to starve our people had been parried by a horrid and strong blow. And over there upon his isle our relentless enemy would receive the same kind of a newspaper notice. The only difference was that there it would cause fury instead of joy, and the dried-up old English editor would stare terrified on the telegram which he would hold in his hand, pull off his few white threads of hair, and swear as only an Englishman can swear.

Even up to the dusk of the night, we towed the sunken freighter's three boats towards the coast. We then cut loose in order to get ready to manœuvre. When darkness set in, one had to be ready for surprises.

Besides, we were not very far from land and the weather was fair, so that the boats could be in no danger. As a refreshment, I had three bottles of wine brought over to the captain of the ill-fated ship, and left him with best greetings to Mr. Churchill and his colleagues.

The last streak of day became paler and paler in the west. The spook-like red cloud-riders stretched themselves more and more, became indistinct, pulled themselves asunder, and at once were swept away. In their place appeared the dark demon of the night, spread itself over heaven, hid all the stars, and settled heavily over the sea.

This was just a night suitable for us. One could not see one's hand before the eye. The steel covers on the tower windows were tightly shut, so that the least ray of light could not escape. Entirely invisible we were gliding forward in the dark. Dumb and immovable, each one was sitting at his post—the lieutenant, the subordinate officer, and the commander—trying with our eyes to pierce through the darkness and turning our heads continually from right to left and back again. The aim of our voyage was still far off and the fine weather had to be used.

Weakly, as if from a far distance, the phonograph's song reached us lonely watchmen:

Reach me thy hand, thy dear hand;
Live well, my treasure, live well!
'Cause we travel now to Eng-eland,
Live well, my treasure, live well,
'Cause we travel now to Eng-eland.

2

An Eventful Night

What peculiar sensations filled me. We were at war—the most insane war ever fought! And now I am a commander on a U-boat!

I said to myself:

"You submarine, you undersea boat, you faithful U-202, which has obediently and faithfully carried me thousands of miles and will still carry me many thousand miles! I am a commander of a submarine which scatters death and destruction in the ranks of the enemy, which carries death and hell fire in its bosom, and which rushes through the water like a thoroughbred. What am I searching for in the cold, dark night? Do I think about honour and success? Why does my eye stare so steadily into the dark? Am I thinking about death and the innumerable mines which are floating away off there in the dark, am I thinking about enemy scouts which are seeking me?

"No! It is nerves and foolish sentiments born of foolish spirits. I am not thinking about that. Leave me alone and don't bother me. I am the master. It is the duty of my nerves to obey. Can you hear the melodious song from below, you weakling nerves? Are you so dull and faint hearted that it does not echo within you? Do you not know the stimulating power which the thin metal voice below can inspire within you?

"This song brings greetings to you from a distance of twelve hundred miles and through twelve hundred miles it comes to you. Ahead we must look; we must force our eyes to pierce the darkness on all sides."

The spy-glass flew to the eye. There is a flash in the west. A light!

"Hey, there! Hey! There is something over there——"

"That is no ordinary light. What about it?"

Lieutenant Petersen was looking through his night glasses at the light.

"I believe he is signalling," he said excitedly. "The light flashes continually to and fro. I hope it is not a scout ship trying to speak with someone."

Hardly had the lieutenant uttered these words when we all three jumped as if electrified, because certainly in our immediate neighbourhood flashed before us several quick lights giving signals, which undoubtedly came from the ship second in line, which was signalling to our first friend.

"Great God! An enemy ship! Not more than three hundred metres ahead!" I exclaimed to myself.

"Hard a starboard! Both engines at highest speed ahead! To the diving stations!"

In a subdued voice, I called my commands down the tower.

The phonograph in the crew-room stopped abruptly. A hasty, eager running was discernible through the entire boat as each one hurried to his post.

The boat immediately obeyed the rudder and was flying to starboard. Between the two hostile ships there was a continuous exchange of signals.

"God be praised it is so dark!" I exclaimed with a deep breath as soon as the first danger had passed.

"And to think that the fellow had to betray his presence by his chattering signals just as we were about to run right into his arms," was the answer. "This time we can truly say that the good God, Himself, had charge of the rudder."

The engineer appeared on the stairway which leads from the "*Centrale*" up to the conning tower.

"May I go to the engine-room, *Herr* Captain-Lieutenant?"

It was not permissible for him to leave his diving station, the "*Centrale*," which is situated in the center of the boat, without special permission.

"Yes, *Herr* Engineer, go ahead down and fire up hard!" I replied.

The thumping of the heavy oil-motors became stronger, swelled higher and higher, and, at last, became a long drawn out roar, and entirely drowned the sound of the occasional jolts which always were distinctly discernible when going at slower speed. One truly felt how the boat exerted its strength to the utmost and did everything within its power.

We had put ourselves on another course which put the anxiously signalling Britishers obliquely aport of our stern, and rushed with the highest speed for about ten minutes until their lights became smaller and weaker. We then turned point by point into our former course, and thus slipped by in a large half circle around the hostile ships.

"Just as a cat around a bowl of hot oatmeal," said Lieutenant Petersen.

"No, my dear friend," I said laughingly, "it does not entirely coincide. The cat always comes back, but the oatmeal is too hot for us in this case. Or do you think that I intend to circle around those two rascals for hours?"

"Preferably not, *Herr* Captain-Lieutenant. It could end badly!"

"Both engines in highest speed forward, let the crew leave the diving stations, place the guards!" I ordered.

The danger had passed. Normal conditions at night could again be resumed. But before the morning set in, we again experienced all kinds of adventures. The night was as if bewitched. There was no sleep worth mentioning. I had hardly, towards ten o'clock, reached my comfortable little nest where the sailor Schultes, our own considerate "cup-bearer," had spread on my miniature writing-desk the most tempting delicacies of preserves and fruit together with a bottle of claret, when a whistle sounded in the speaking-tube on the wall right close to my head:

"Whee-e!" it shrieked, high, penetrating and alarming.

I jumped up, pulled out the stopper and put in the mouth-piece. "Hello!"

"Two points from starboard a white light!"

I grabbed my cap and gloves and rushed sternward through the deck officer's room, petty officer's room, and crew-room, each one narrower than the other.

"Look out, the commander!" they shouted to one another, and pulled in their legs so that I could get by.

"Ouch!" I bumped my head hard against the stand of an electric lamp. I rubbed the sore spot as I hurried ahead, while I took an oath to myself that the lamp should be moved at the first possible opportunity. I hurried through the "*Centrale*," up the narrow stairway. Then I reached my place.

"Where?"

"There!" Lieutenant Gröning, who was on guard, pointed out. "About three points starboard!"

"It is a steamer. One can already see the red side lantern. It is crossing our course."

I put my binoculars to the eye and looked for many seconds for the light. The officer on guard was right. Besides the white lantern, one could see a deep, red light. The ship therefore was traveling towards the left and would cross our course.

A narrow strip of the moon had appeared from out of the sea and was wrestling with the darkness of the night. The result was not much—the strip of the moon was too small for that—still it was not so dark as before.

"Don't let it come too close to us!" I ordered. "And get clear in right time. We must not under any circumstances be seen by it, because then they would soon know in England from which direction to expect us. Now nearly every steamer has a wireless."

Gröning changed the course to port until he had the steamer completely to the left.

"Too bad, we can't take it with us," he said.

"No, you know, for a night attack this is not the right place. Here so many neutral steamers travel, and an error can easily be made."

It was shortly after ten o'clock. At eleven-twenty, twelve forty, one-ten, three-fifteen, and five o'clock I again heard the whistling "Whee-e!" in the speaking-tube by my bunk. Each time I had to jump out of some dream, realize within a fraction of a second that my presence was desired up-stairs, grab my cap and gloves, and rush through the boat's long body up to the tower, not without several times bumping into the aforementioned and often damned electric lamp.

After five o'clock in the morning I remained on deck, because dawn would soon break with its treacherous light. The commander's post is in the tower at such a time because, just as easily as one perceives in the pale gray light a ship, one is also visible from the steamer, which could cause many unpleasant surprises if the two ships are not very cordial towards each other—especially disagreeable to us because a submarine is, as our name indicates, below the water, and the smallest fragment of a shell can badly damage our heel of Achilles, the diving machinery, so that we would be unable again to get into a position of safety beneath the surface.

Shortly before six o'clock I had the entire crew at the diving stations. Each took his place, ready at a given command to open or shut the valve, crank, or bolt of which he had charge. Only the cook had no special duty besides his own. He remained with the electric cooking apparatus provided in the galley and had no other job besides taking care of our bodily comfort. Now he was, in conformity with his duty, busy making coffee as was proper at that time of day.

A fine, strong smell of coffee percolated through the whole ship, which proved to be a great stimulant to our taut nerves and our empty stomachs.

I have to deviate a little from the subject for the purpose of asking if my readers understand me. Is it above all plain, explicit, and clear why I give so much space to a discussion of the nerves when I speak about us, U-boat men, and so often refer to them? The nerves are in time of peace the Alpha and Omega for a U-boat officer. How much more so when we are at war! The nerves to us mean power to act, decision, strength, will, and perseverance. The nerves are valuable and to keep them in good condition is of the greatest importance and an obligation and duty during a voyage.

There we sit hour after hour in the conning tower. Beneath is the most complicated mechanism the genius of man has ever created. And all around there are the most craftily constructed instruments for the purpose of destroying that which cost so much labour to create. Mines, nets, explosives, shells, and sharp keels are our enemies, which, at any moment, may send us high in the air or hundreds of metres into the ocean. Everywhere perils lurk. The whole sea is a powder barrel.

For all this there is only one remedy—nerves!

To make the right decision at the right moment is the first and last of U-boat science. One glance must be enough to determine the position. In the same second a decision must be made, and the commands carried out. A moment's hesitation may be fatal.

I can give an example of this on the very morning I speak of.

It was three minutes after six o'clock, and within about half an hour the sun would rise, but the sea and the sky still floated together in the colourless drab of early dawn and permitted one only to imagine, not see, that partition wall, the horizon.

Unceasingly our binoculars pierced the gray dusk of daybreak. Suddenly a shiver went through my body when—only a second immovable and in intense suspense—a dark shadow within range of the spy-glass made me jump. The shadow grew and became larger, like a giant on the horizon—one mast; one, two, three, four funnels—a destroyer.

A quick command—I leap down into the tower. The water rushes into the diving tanks. The conning tower covers slam tight behind me—and the agony which follows tries our patience, while we count seconds with watches in hand until the tanks are filled, and the boat slips below the sea.

Never in my life did a second seem so long to me. The destroyer, which is not more than two thousand metres distant from us, has, of course, seen us, and is speeding for us as fast as her forty thousand horse power can drive her. From the guns mounted on her bow flash one shot after another aimed to destroy us.

Good God! If he only does not hit! Just one little hit, and we are lost! Already the water splashes on the outside of the conning tower up to the glass windows through which I see the dark ghost, streaking straight for us. It is terrifying to hear the shells bursting all around us in the water. It sounds like a trip-hammer against a steel plate, and closer and closer come the metallic crashes. The rascal is getting our range.

There—the fifth shot—the entire boat trembles—then the deceitful daylight disappears from the conning tower window. The boat obeys the diving rudder and submerges into the sea.

A reddish-yellow light shines all around us; the indicator of the manometer, which measures our depth, points to eight metres, nine metres, ten metres, twelve metres. Saved!

What a happy, unexplainable sensation to know that you are hiding deep in the infinite ocean! The heart, which had stopped beating during these long seconds because it had no time to beat, again begins its pounding.

Our boat sinks deeper and deeper. It obeys, as does a faithful horse the slightest pressure of a rider's knees, which, in this case, are the diving rudders placed in the bow and the stern. The manometer now shows twenty-four metres, twenty-six metres. I had given orders we should go down to thirty metres.

Above us we still hear the roaring and crackling in the water, as if it were in an impotent rage. I turn and smile at the mate who is standing with me in the conning tower—a happy, care-free smile. I point upwards with my thumb.

"Do you hear it? Do you hear it?"

It is an unnecessary question, of course, because he hears it as plainly as I do, and all the others aboard hear it, too. But the question can still be explained because of the tremendous strain on our nerves which has to express itself even in such a simple question.

Dear, true, splendid little boat, how one learns to love you during such trying moments and would like to pet you like a living human being for your understanding and obedience! We, here on board, all depend upon you, just as we all depend upon one another. We are chained together. We will face the dangers together and gain success.

You blond heroes who are standing down there in the bowels of the boat without knowing what is happening up in the light, but still knowing that the crucial moment has arrived—that life or death to everyone depends on one man's will and one man's decision; you who, with a calm and strong feeling of duty, stick at your posts with all the strength of your bodies and souls strained to the breaking point and still keep full faith in him who is your leader, chief, and commander; you show the highest degree of bravery and self-control, you who never have a chance to see the enemy but still, with sustained calm, do your duty.

Not a word was uttered, not a sound disturbed that deadly stillness on board. One almost forgot that the men were standing with strained nerves at their posts in order to keep the wonderful mechanism running right. One could hear the soft whirr of the dynamos and, more and more distant, the crackling of the exploding shells. Suddenly even this stopped. The Britisher must have noticed that the fish had slipped out of his hand. Shortly thereafter we heard his propellers churning the water above us. Soon this noise died away as it had come, growing fainter and fainter in a kind of grinding whirr.

"Did you hear how he circled around over us?" I asked through the speaking tube which led down into the "*Centrale*."

"Certainly. That could clearly be distinguished," was the short answer.

I was pondering over what to do next. At first we had no choice but to dive at the first sight of the destroyer suddenly appearing with the break of day.

In our capacity as an undersea boat, we were now in a position to fight on equal terms, and I decided to risk a bout with him as soon as it became light enough for me to see through the periscope. The intervening time I made use of by having passed up to me in the tower the long desired cup of morning coffee, in order to stop the tantalizing agony which the smell of the coffee had caused my empty stomach. Thereupon we slowly climbed upwards from our safe breakfast depth of thirty metres. The higher we came—one can read on the manometer how we are ascending metre by metre—the greater became the excitement and tension. Without breathing we listened.

Slowly the boat rose. The top of the periscope would soon be thrust above the surface. My hands clasped the handle with which the well-oiled, and therefore easily movable, periscope can be turned around as quickly as lightning, in order to take a sweep around the horizon. My eye was pressed to the sight, and soon I perceived that the water was getting clearer and clearer by degrees and more transparent. I could now follow the ascent of the boat without consulting the manometer.

My heart was pounding with the huntsman's fervour, in expectation of what I was to see at my first quick glance around the horizon, because the destroyer, which we sighted only a quarter of an hour before, could be only a scouting ship. It might belong to a detachment of naval scouts to protect a larger ship. In my thoughts I saw the whole eastern horizon full of proud ships under England's flag surrounded by smoke. I did not see anything, no matter how carefully I scanned the horizon. All I could see was the reddening morning blush spread over half of the eastern sky, the last stars now paling and the rising sun showing its first beams.

"For heaven's sake, nobody is here," I grumbled to myself.

"Oh, he'll surely come back, Captain," said my mate with true optimism. "The prey was too hot for him to tackle and now he has started to fetch a couple more to help him."

"It would certainly be less desirable," put in Lieutenant Gröning, who, full of expectations, was standing halfway up the stairway leading from the tower to the "*Centrale*" and had overheard our talk. "No, it would be less desirable," he repeated, "because then comes the entire swarm of hostile U-boats with their nets cunningly lined with mines. No good will ever come of that."

"There you are right, Gröning," I agreed. "With that sort of a nuisance, equipped as they are with so many machines for our destruction, it would be very disagreeable to make their acquaintance. If they come, it is best to disappear. It is not worth the risk. We have many more important duties ahead of us. It would be too bad to spoil a good torpedo on such trash."

At the same time, I decided to rise so as to get a better observation through the periscope and once more look around the horizon. I suddenly observed in the northeast a peculiar, dark cloud of smoke. I, therefore, did not give any orders to arise, but told "*Centrale*" by a few short commands through the speaking tube the new turn of affairs and, with added speed, went to meet the smoke cloud.

3

The Sinking of the Transport

Soon the outlines of a ship told us that ahead of us was a large steamer, steaming westward at high speed. The disappointment which we experienced at first was soon reversed when it was clearly shown that the fortunes of war had again sent a ship across our course which belonged to a hostile power.

No flag could be seen—nor was it run up. Otherwise we would have seen it.

"This is a suspicious circumstance," I reasoned with myself.

I called down to the "*Centrale*" all my observations through the periscope at regular intervals, snapping them out in the same sharp, brief style that the newsboys use in calling out the headlines to the listening public. My words were passed in whispers from mouth to mouth until all hands on board knew what was going on above the surface. Each new announcement from the conning tower caused great excitement among the crew, listening and holding their breath and, I believe, if you could measure the tension on human nerves with a barometer, it would have registered to the end of the tube, when, like hammer beats, these words went down to the "*Centrale*":

"The steamer's armed! Take a look, mate."

I stepped away from the sights of the periscope. "Can you see the gun mounted forward of the bridge?"

"Yes, certainly," he replied excitedly. "I can see it, and quite a large piece it is, too."

"Now take a look at her stern—right by the second mast—what do you notice there?"

"Thousand devils! Another cannon—at least a ten-centimetre gun. It's a transport, sure."

"Drop the periscope! Port ten!" I commanded.

185

"Torpedo tube ready!" reported the torpedo master through the tube from the forward torpedo compartment.

By this time I had the periscope submerged so that we were completely below the surface and out of sight, and it would be impossible to discover us from the steamer, even after the most careful searching of the horizon.

"Advance on the enemy!" was our determination.

Oh, what a glorious sensation is a U-boat attack! What a great understanding and co-operation between a U-boat and its crew—between dead matter and living beings! What a merging into a single being, of the nerves and spirits of an entire crew!

"Just as if the whole boat is as one being," was the thought that passed through my mind when I, with periscope down, went at my antagonist, just like a great crouching cat with her back bowed and her hair on end, ready to spring. The eye is the periscope, the brain the conning tower, the heart the "*Centrale*," the legs the engines, and the teeth and claws the torpedoes.

Noiselessly we slipped closer and closer in our exciting chase. The main thing was that our periscope should not be observed, or the steamer might change her course at the last moment and escape us. Very cautiously, I stuck just the tip of the periscope above the surface at intervals of a few minutes, took the position of the steamer in a second and, like a flash, pulled it down again. That second was sufficient for me to see what I wanted to see. The steamer was to starboard and was heading at a good speed across our bows. To judge from the foaming waves which were cut off from the bow, I calculated that her speed must be about sixteen knots.

The hunter knows how important it is to have a knowledge of the speed at which his prey is moving. He can calculate the speed a little closer when it is a wounded hare than when it is one which in flight rushes past at high speed.

It was only necessary for me, therefore, to calculate the speed of the ship for which a sailor has an experienced eye. I then plotted the exact angle we needed. I measured this by a scale which had been placed above the sights of the periscope. Now I only had to let the steamer come along until it had reached the zero point on the periscope and fire the torpedo, which then must strike its mark.

You see, it is very plain; I estimate the speed of the boat, aim with the periscope and fire at the right moment.

He who wishes to know about this or anything else in this connection should join the navy, or if he is not able to do so, send us his son or brother or nephew.

On the occasion in question everything went as calculated. The steamer could not see our cautious and hardly-shown periscope and continued unconcerned on its course. The diving rudder in the "*Centrale*" worked well and greatly facilitated my unobserved approach. I could clearly distinguish the various objects on board, and saw the giant steamer at a very short distance—how the captain was walking back and forth on the bridge with a short pipe in his mouth, how the crew was scrubbing the forward deck. I saw with amazement—a shiver went through me—a long line of compartments of wood spread over the entire deck, out of which were sticking black and brown horse heads and necks.

Oh, great Scott! Horses! What a pity! Splendid animals!

"What has that to do with it?" I continually thought. War is war. And every horse less on the western front is to lessen England's defence. I have to admit, however, that the thought which had to come was disgusting, and I wish to make the story about it short.

Only a few degrees were lacking for the desired angle, and soon the steamer would get into the correct focus. It was passing us at the right distance, a few hundred metres.

"Torpedo ready!" I called down into the "*Centrale*."

It was the longed-for command. Everyone on board held his breath. Now the steamer's bow cut the line in the periscope—now the deck, the bridge, the foremast—the funnel.

"Let go!"

A light trembling shook the boat—the torpedo was on its way. Woe, when it was let loose!

There it was speeding, the murderous projectile, with an insane speed straight at its prey. I could accurately follow its path by the light wake it left in the water.

"Twenty seconds," counted the mate whose duty it was, with watch in hand, to calculate the exact time elapsed after the torpedo was fired until it exploded.

"Twenty-two seconds!"

Now it must happen—the terrible thing!

I saw the ship's people on the bridge had discovered the wake which the torpedo was leaving, a slender stripe. How they pointed with their fingers out across the sea in terror; how the captain, covering his face with his hands, resigned himself to what must come. And next there was a terrific shaking so that all aboard the steamer were tossed about and then, like a volcano, arose, majestic but fearful in its beauty, a two-hundred metre high and fifty-meter wide pillar of water toward the sky.

"A full hit behind the second funnel!" I called down into the "*Centrale.*" Then they cut loose down there for joy. They were carried away by ecstasy which welled out of their hearts, a joyous storm that ran through our entire boat and up to me.

And over there?

Landlubber, steel thy heart!

A terrible drama was being enacted on the hard-hit sinking ship. It listed and sank towards us.

From the tower I could observe all the decks. From all the hatches human beings forced their way out, fighting despairingly. Russian firemen, officers, sailors, soldiers, hostlers, the kitchen crew, all were running and calling for the boats. Panic stricken, they thronged about one another down the stairways, fighting for the lifeboats, and among all were the rearing, snorting and kicking horses. The boats on the starboard deck could not be put into service, as they could not be swung clear because of the list of the careening steamer. All, therefore, thronged to the boats on the port side, which, in the haste and anguish, were lowered, some half empty; others overcrowded. Those who were left aboard were wringing their hands in despair. They ran from bow to stern and back again from stern to bow in their terror, and then finally threw themselves into the sea in order to attempt to swim to the boats.

Then another explosion resounded, after which a hissing white wave of steam streamed out of all the ports. The hot steam set the horses crazy, and they were beside themselves with terror—I could see a splendid, dapple-gray horse with a long tail make a great leap over the ship's side and land in a lifeboat, already overcrowded—but after that I could not endure the terrible spectacle any longer. Pulling down the periscope, we submerged into the deep.

When, after some time, I came again to the surface there was nothing more to be seen of the great, proud steamer. Among the wreckage and corpses of the horses three boats were floating and occasionally fished out a man still swimming in the sea. Now I came up on the surface in order to assist the victims of the wrecked ship. When our boat's mighty, whale-like hull suddenly arose out of the water, right in their midst, a panic seized them again and quickly they grasped their oars in order to try to flee. Not until I waved from the tower to them with my handkerchief and cap did they rest on their oars and come over to us. The state in which some of them were was exceedingly pitiful. Several wore only white cotton trousers and had handkerchiefs wrapped around their necks. The fixed provisions which each boat was required to carry were not sufficient when the boat's crew was doubled and trebled.

While I was conferring with our mess officer as to what we could possibly dispense with of our own provisions we noticed to the north and west some clouds of smoke which, to judge from the signs, were coming towards us quickly. Immediately a thought flashed through my head:

"Now they are looking for you. Now comes the whole swarm."

Already the typical masts of the British destroyers and trawlers arose above the horizon. We, therefore, did not have a minute to lose in order to escape these hostile and most dangerous enemies. I made my decision quickly and called to the captain of the sunken steamer that he could let one of the oncoming ships pick them up as I could not spare the time, but had to go "northeast." Then I submerged—right in front of the boats full of survivors. They saw me head north and I steered in that direction for a time. Then I pulled down the periscope and, without being noticed, changed my course to the south.

When I, after a considerable time, again cautiously looked around, I perceived to my amazement that an entire scout fleet in a wide circle was heading towards us from the south also. From three sides the enemy spurred his bloodhounds on us, and I thought to myself it would not take long before, by extending their wings, they would encircle us completely, and the great chase would begin. The thought was not cheerful, particularly as the depths in this part of the ocean were not sufficient so that we could, by submerging deeply, guard ourselves against the dangers of grappling hooks, nets and mines.

"The wildcat has become a hare," I thought to myself and, at the same time, I decided what to do.

We had to do as the old hare. First, with eyes open, we would cautiously jump forth, use all possible covers, and search for the spot where the gunners were fewest, and then with eyes shut and at the highest possible speed break through the widest gap.

Consequently, we began to travel toward the east where the "atmosphere was still clear." Occasionally I stuck up my periscope and perceived how the surrounding circle was knit tighter and tighter.

Now, after I had made up my mind, I became completely calm and carefully considered all the conditions for and against us. The swarm of destroyers moved toward the center, as in a regular chase, as soon as the circle was complete. Between every couple of hunters—I mean trawlers—there were nets stretched across to catch a little submarine, and behind these were dragged mines.

By extending one of the wings in the north, it made a gap toward the east, and besides I saw that one of the torpedo boats between two groups of the searching parties had left for the shipwrecked survivors. At this point, consequently, was our best chance to escape. I laid my course between the two searching parties, of course, with the periscope, during the whole time, nearly invisible.

Slowly the ranks of the hunting hounds approached, smoking copiously and snorting. Now the right moment had arrived to follow the other part of the hare's program. We shut our eyes—that is, I pulled the periscope down completely—and proceeded with increased speed, submerging in the sea as deeply as possible.

I can well imagine how the old hare felt when he ran blindly for his life. Undoubtedly our feelings were somewhat the same. How easily could not that little gap toward which we were making be closed by some small auxiliary of the searchers.

And, if the grappling hooks from one of these got hold of us, there would be little hope of escape, or of saving ourselves. Then they would tear at us from all directions and give us the stab that would send us deep down into the sea for good. No one on board suspected what danger we went to meet. I had kept all my observations concerning the enemy's surrounding us to myself and had not mentioned it, so as not to excite everybody's mind. No one below could at any rate do anything to change the conditions.

Then from the bow compartment came the report:

"The beating of propellers is discernible to port!"

Shortly thereafter I could hear them, even from the conning tower—a soft, slow, swelling, and grinding sound. This was not the sound of the propellers of a destroyer. Such would beat faster, clearer, and more powerfully. This was the heavily-dragging trawlers' slow beating propellers.

Strainingly I listened to starboard—nothing could be heard. That was a good sign, because I could hope that in reality I had reached the gap and that the sounds of the propellers which we heard to port emanated from the trawler on the left side of the gap. I was just about, from my innermost heart, to let out a joyous "hurrah," when, from the bow of the boat, I heard a new sound which approached with a clear, sharp banging. It was the torpedo-boat, the beast! Was the rascal going to come back at the crucial moment?

It required only a few seconds for the torpedo-boat to pass over us, but those seemed as hours. At every blinking of the eye I imagined I heard something explode, turn against or drag alongside my boat. But fortune was ours. The sharp, grinding sound of the swift torpedo-boat propellers became fainter and fainter and, at last, ceased entirely. Unconsciously I straightened up a little in the tower, whistled a few notes from "*Dockan*," and tapped, as if nothing had happened, with the knuckle of my forefinger on the glass of the manometer. What did the manometer register? Nothing whatsoever had happened. Everything was in the best condition. The depth coincided. The diving rudder was lying normal. Before me stood Tuczynski, my faithful helmsman and orderly, at former times skipper on the *Weichsel* and *Nogat*; behind me, the mate leaned against the wall of the conning tower contentedly and yawned.

I suddenly felt an unresistible craving for a cigarette. The nerves needed some stimulation. For about ten minutes I controlled myself. Then I arose to a periscope distance from the surface and took a look around to see how things were going. What I saw filled my heart with joy. The whole swarm of British destroyers and trawlers had moved toward the southwest and were eagerly searching in a long line. As we were proceeding in an opposite direction we quickly left them. After about five more minutes I would dare to come to the surface. To the north the way was clear.

Soon I was sitting, in the best of spirits, up in the conning tower, greedily inhaling with both lungs the fine, refreshing sea air and, mixed with it, the long puffs of the cigarette.

4

Rich Spoils

Late in the afternoon of the same day we broke into a peacefully working fishing flotilla just like a wolf into a flock of sheep. In order to be sure no shepherd with his dog was guarding them we, keeping ourselves submerged, carefully examined each ship. I could not see a gun or anything suspicious anywhere.

All were peacefully occupied at their casting nets, fishing. There were seven fishing steamers and nine sailing ships, which were scattered over a distance of about three miles. The weather was glorious, even better than the day before. The sun smiled from a steel blue sky and danced in golden stripes on the bright, calm surface of the sea. A gentle northerly swell rocked the fishing boats back and forth, so that the gaffs and the frames on which the extra nets had been stretched to dry were swinging and banging.

Countless numbers of sea gulls were flying about close to the flotilla. With shrill cries and in thick flocks, they swooped down on the sterns of some isolated boats, and hurled themselves, gliding on their wings, into the refuse of the last catch which the fishermen were throwing overboard.

The horizon stood out visibly from the sea all around and seemed to be a great shining, glittering ring. Not a speck of cloud spotted its bright edges. Nothing was visible except our fishermen.

Hurrah, this was just the weather for us! A rare and favourable opportunity had presented itself here to play a trick on the English fish market.

As a ghost, I suddenly arose behind one of the fishing steamers, pushed the conning tower hatch up, and jumped up on the tower, holding the flag of war in one hand and the megaphone in the other.

"Halloo-o-o!"

The fishermen stared at us open mouthed, rooted to the spot as if paralyzed by fear of us.

"Halloo-o-o-o, Captain!" I shouted for the second time. "I want to talk to you."

After some time a figure emerged from the crowd, stepped up the stairway, and shouted some words that were not very clear but which sounded like:

"Here I am!"

I summoned my best English and told the red-nosed chap that I would have to sink before sundown the whole fleet of fishing boats, and furthermore I told him that I had selected him to take the crews of all the others aboard his steamer. I added he must immediately cut his nets and follow me at a distance of five hundred metres, and that I would promptly blow him to pieces if he, of his own accord, attempted to diminish this distance as I would then surely believe he intended to ram me.

The captain declared he was willing to obey my commands, cut the nets, and followed me. I ordered full speed ahead and hoisted to the mast the following signal:

"Leave the boat immediately!"

Then I rushed in among the excited swarm. With flashing eyes, the sailors were standing by our guns and waiting, lovingly fondling the shells, ready to begin firing.

First we went right through the crowd of fishing-boats and then along the edges of the fleet, in order to prevent the escape of the steamers furthest away. Nowhere did we take the time to stop to sink a ship, but only drove the crews away from their boats. Then the prey could not get away from us.

How promptly the fishermen alighted because of the fear of our shells! They scrambled aboard the one steamer selected to save them in such a rush it looked like a panicky flight. Soon cutters and row-boats were swarming all around us and speedily the steamer selected to save the crews was crowded.

But even during such an exciting occupation we did not neglect to keep a sharp lookout, for under no circumstances were we to be taken by surprise when at this work. But it was easy to look out over a great distance. The horizon was free and clear.

As soon as the fishermen were safe aboard the steamer, we began the sinking of the ships and went from ship to ship, stopped at a distance of a hundred metres, and sent solid, well-aimed shots at their water lines until they had had enough and began to sink. Many went down with the first shot. Others were tougher and required four. For the gun crew this was great sport. They took turns and each jealously counted the number of shots required for his "fisherman."

When the steamers were "fixed," we went to the sailing boats, which, in accordance with their inveterate custom, were lying huddled together. The sailors generally needed only one shot—then they capsized and sank into the sea with a death gurgle. It was a touching scene which, in spite of our inner joy, was hard on our nerves, as every true sailor regards the sailing-ship as a remnant of romance, dying out faster and faster in these days.

This was truly the reason why now and at other times our hearts ached for each sailing ship which we had to sink. The surface was covered with hundreds of thousands of dead fish which were scattered over the sea. To countless sea gulls it was a highly welcome call to dinner, which they eagerly accepted, gorging themselves and filling themselves so that their feathers stood straight out from their bodies.

We had already sent thirteen ships to the bottom, only two sailing-ships remaining besides the rescue steamer. As the opportunity was a rare one, I permitted the firemen and men from the engine room to come up on deck so that they could see with their own eyes a ship go down. I enjoyed hearing their funny remarks and to watch how, in their childish joy, they enthusiastically greeted each new shot. I was glad to see the bright colour the fresh air and excitement brought to their pale faces. Gröning stepped up to me and said thoughtfully:

"What will happen if the steamer goes to England and tells our position? Following the events of yesterday afternoon, this morning and now, the English can easily figure out our course."

"By Jove, you are right there! I had not happened to think of that. It is indeed true that one gets duller as the years go by. That must be prevented under all circumstances, especially on account of tomorrow. You know what then—don't you?"

Gröning nodded.

"Yes, tomorrow we'll have a trying day," I continued, "and, if we are going to succeed, we can't make conditions any harder for ourselves."

I was pondering the question of how we were going to avoid the danger of being betrayed by the fishermen without endangering their lives, which I did not want to do. I thought this over for a moment. Suddenly I struck my forehead with my hand and laughed.

"So stupidly foolish! One is never able to think of the simplest way!" I said. "We'll simply shift the entire crowd to one of the sailing-ships. With this light breeze, it will take them at least three days to reach the coast and, after that, it does not matter. It will be a little crowded for so many people, but that can't be helped."

"And the provisions?" Gröning asked. "What are they going to live on?"

"That's simple," I answered. "First of all they can take off all the provisions from the steamer and, besides that, they have all the fish in the sailing-ship."

I sank the smaller of the two sailboats and then approached the steamer which had taken aboard the crews from the other boats.

The captain of the steamer was bitterly disappointed, of course, when I brought him word that all hands would have to go to the sailboat. He had been so delighted to be the one chosen to keep his steamer. On the other hand, to the captain of the sailing-ship, the message that he could go back to his old, faithful smack came as a gift from heaven.

Yes, indeed, joy and sorrow lie close together and go hand in hand.

After a short half hour the shift was made, and the steamer also went down into the deep—the fifteenth ship within two hours. First the skipper carefully hauled up his nets and then with flapping sails slowly swung around and laid his course toward the west.

During the night we dropped down to the bottom of the ocean at X——. We wanted to get some rest for one night and gather strength for the next day. It is comfortable to lie in the soft sands of the North Sea. It is as if the whole boat went to bed. One thing necessary for this comfort was a calm surface, because a heavy sea is felt at a great depth and throws and bangs the boat back and forth on the bottom.

Slowly the boat slipped deeper and deeper. We had taken soundings before submerging. The nearer we came to the bottom the slower the dynamo motors worked, and I at last stopped them entirely when we were a few metres from the bottom. As soon as we had stopped sinking, which could be told by the fact the diving rudder was no longer working, a few litres of water were pumped into a ballast tank made for just this purpose. The boat became heavier and slowly sunk further.

"Now, we'll soon strike," I called down to the "*Centrale*" and looked at the manometer.

Hardly had the words left my lips when we felt a very gentle shock—much weaker than when a train stops—and knew we were at the bottom. Some more water was pumped into the ballast tanks in order to make the boat steadier and then each one at his post carefully examined scuttles and hatchways so that not a drop of water could leak through to us. From bow to stern it was reported:

"All is tight!"

Thereafter orders were given for the necessary guards, and then I let the crew leave their posts:

"All hands to be free tonight!"

Until tomorrow on the bottom of the ocean! No other restfulness can be compared with it. Rest after so much excitement which has stirred the emotions of us all; after such a day's work, is it possible that anyone can appreciate how we enjoyed ourselves?

We did not care that we were not in port and that a mountain of ocean was over our heads. We felt as secure as if we had been at the safest spot in the world. From their posts the crew went past us, with pale, oily, and dirty faces, but with their eyes looking at me as they went by, proud, happy, radiant, so that my heart rejoiced.

There was some excitement among the crew. Every one washed, talked and laughed so that it was evident how happy and care-free they felt.

"Well, with what will you treat us today?" I asked the cook who, with great self-confidence—because he was an expert in his line—was standing before his little galley and stirring a steaming pot. "That smells wonderfully appetizing."

"Ox *goulash* and salt potatoes," answered the cook and with more eagerness stirred his pot. "It soon will be ready. It'll not take more than five minutes."

"Then I must hurry up," I replied, and went to my small cabin, where I had not put foot since five o'clock in the morning.

I put my cap, long scarf and oil-skin jacket on a hook, stretched myself in weary delight and washed myself energetically. This is a rare pleasure on a trip like ours. From the nearby room the happy talk of the officers reached my ears. I then heard a rattle of plates and forks, a cork popped from a bottle, and Gröning opened the little door that separates my cabin from the room of the other officers.

"*Herr* Captain, dinner is ready," he said.

Soon we were sitting, four men in all, at a little, nicely decorated table, cutting into the steaming platter and drinking out of small *seidels* a magnificent sparkling wine. The past day's events had to be moistened a little with the best we had. This was our custom when the fortunes of war smiled graciously on us.

The electrical heating apparatus furnishes all the heat needed, but it still has the disadvantage that in the still, unchanged air, the heat arises so that the temperature at the floor is several degrees colder than at the ceiling. Even in our heavy sea-boots, we felt it a little, although, as a whole, we were warm and contented. The phonograph played continuously. The petty officers had taken charge of it and played one native song after another. What a thrill ran through me! At once there was silence. All talk stopped. German songs of the Fatherland were sung deep down at the bottom of the ocean right on England's coast. Inspired by the music, our hearts were filled with enthusiasm and a silent promise was made to give everything for the Fatherland—to become a scourge to the enemy and damage him with all our might.

Thereafter, the dance music, operettas, vaudeville songs, and ragtime were played. These stirred up a buoyant spirit. Especially there was much joy among the firemen and sailors in the crew's quarters. Funny songs could be heard from that direction. Dirty playing cards were dug out and soon there was a real German *skat* game in full swing.

During this time we, in the officers' mess, raised our glasses and drank toasts to one another and to the beautiful U-boat: "Rich spoils! A happy journey home! Long live the U-boat!" That is the U-boat toast.

The boat was lying very still. It didn't seem to stir.

"What an original idea for an artist!" said our engineer, who was poetically inclined, as he leaned back in his chair staring thoughtfully at the ceiling. "One can imagine a cross section of the boat showing our room at the North Sea's yellowish sand bottom, to which all kinds of crawling and swimming animals give life. In here four feasting, happy officers around a little table on which a warm electric light is shining with the wine bottle in the center and with the glasses raised to a solemn toast. Above—water, water, water—water to the height of a church steeple and, over it all, the glittering heavens full of stars and a small silver-white piece of the moon. If I were a painter I should immediately start with this motive for a picture."

"And give me the picture, I hope," I laughed. "And, after all, not such a bad idea about that picture—one should in reality propose such a motive to an artist."

"Maybe it would be possible to put in a couple of mermaids who look in through the conning tower window inquisitively and knock with their fingers on the glass," said Petersen, our youngest lieutenant, with a smile. "That would undoubtedly make the picture still more attractive."

Gröning, who during the entire time had listened with a quiet smile to the conversation, took out his empty cigar holder, on which he always chewed when we were under water because, as a heavy smoker, he missed tobacco, as none of us was allowed to smoke inside the boat. Slowly he said with a touch of irony, in a deep, sympathetic voice:

"Here, my dear Petersen, you are an unreasonable rascal. If there are no women in the game, then there is no pleasure for you. Doesn't the fellow actually talk about mermaids when he tells us every fourth week he is going to become engaged. 'This time it's absolutely certain! This time I surely will do it, as I will never find such a girl again.' This and more I hear every month. What was the last one's name that you intended to make happy—your March girl? Wait, I have it—the February girl—ha, ha, ha—has the captain heard the story of the February girl?"

He turned to me laughing.

"Will you shut up, Gröning!" Petersen burst forth and blushed up to his ears. "I'll tell you that if you tell tales out of school—and besides——"

"Well, Petersen," I encouraged, "what 'besides'?"

"Besides, all that is not true," he continued and blushed still more when he noticed that he had betrayed himself. "*You* should certainly keep quiet," he went on suddenly, beaming with an idea, and began to attack in order to lead the conversation away from himself. "He who lives in glass houses should be more careful."

"I—I—I—how so—that's the limit!" Gröning angrily rejoined, as he considered it an honor to be known among his friends as a woman hater. "I—in a glass house? It's a mean accusation, or have you been drinking too much wine, my dear boy?"

"Bah! Only a glass," answered the younger officer, defending himself. "It is ridiculous to claim anything like that."

"Well, well, be friends now, sirs," I said soothingly. "Don't let's quarrel down here at the bottom of the sea. I hereby decide that our younger officer is absolutely sober, but that, even so, he will not be allowed to let his April girl with her fishtail come in here, as a punishment, because he has jilted his February girl."

With this decision both these fighting roosters (really the best friends in the world) had to be pleased, and the eternal discussion of Eve and her daughters, which had nearly made the ocean bottom shake under our feet, was ended.

Shortly after this we went to bed in our narrow bunks—for the first time undressed on the voyage—and soon enjoyed a sleep free from dreams.

5

The Witch-Kettle

In the morning no rooster crowed to wake me. But, instead, there stood my faithful orderly, the Pole, Tuczynski, before my bed, and loudly announced:

"*Herr* Captain Lieutenant, it's five-thirty!"

I woke up in bewilderment. My head was still dull after a sound sleep.

"What's up?"

"It's five-thirty," repeated the orderly. "The water for washing and the clothes are ready."

Ah! Like a flash the reality was before me. We were lying on the bottom of the sea—were going to arise within an hour—and then we were going to——

I leaped out of bed. The thought of "then we were going to" fully awoke me. "Yes, we are going to go at it; everything depends upon today," I thought, and put my feet into my slippers.

Hardly had I scrambled to my feet when I had to grasp the closet to support myself.

"What's up now?" I asked, turning to my good Pole, who was spitting on my left boot in order to preserve the shine. "We are rolling. What's happened?"

"Must be a little sea above," he replied with a grin.

"I can understand that myself, you smarty, but when did it start? Run along quickly and find out when the rolling was first noticed!"

Tuczynski hurried to the "*Centrale*" and returned immediately with his answer:

"About two o'clock, says Lieutenant Petersen."

"Well, then we must have a considerable storm above, if the wind has been blowing for four hours. Get out my oil-skin coat quickly!

200

It will be needed today," I ordered, and hurriedly dressed myself as water-tight as possible.

The change of weather did not suit my purpose, for, although to judge from the motion of the boat the storm was not as yet so bad, the strength of the wind was probably six, and it was gradually becoming worse. At this time of the year storms could be terrible.

"Devil take the luck—and this very day, too!" I swore through my six-day old beard-stub.

After breakfast I called the entire crew together. "Boys," I said, "you know that we have many things unaccomplished. As yet we are only at the beginning of our task. Yesterday and the day before we were very successful, and now we have had a restful night. Being well rested, we are now cheerfully and confidently ready for another day's work. Today we are going to go through the so-called 'Witch-Kettle.' You all know what I mean, and you know also that this is not child's play. The enemy there is keeping sharp lookout, but we will keep a better lookout. Others have gotten through before us. Consequently, we will also get through, if each one of you sticks to his post and does his duty as well as you all have done hitherto. This I expect from every man. And now—to the diving stations!"

I went up to the tower. Shortly after the engineer reported from the "*Centrale*":

"All hands are at the diving station!"

Consequently we were ready for our task. The day began—the most remarkable day of my life.

"Arise!"

The pump began to buzz. We now had to empty the ballast-tanks of the water which had been taken in to make the boat heavier, in order that, instead of being held down, we should begin to pull ourselves loose, and drift slowly upwards. Usually that manœuvre was accomplished with the best of success, but not so today. The boat wobbled and "stuck," as we used to say. It called to my mind the question which is often asked by laymen: "Are you never in fear of not being able to get up to the surface again?" We, of course, had no fear, but I knocked impatiently on the manometer to see if the register would not at last begin to move.

"Nine hundred litres above the normal," Krüger reported from the "*Centrale*."

It meant that we had pumped out of the boat nine hundred litres more than the normal quantity necessary to make the boat rise.

"It seems as if we were fastened in a vice," I joked, "but in accordance with the map there ought to be a sand bottom here."

"Now it loosens!" the engineer called out.

Yes, the boat pulled loose all right—the hand on the manometer was rising—but it shot upwards on one side only. The stern arose but the nose remained fastened in the mud.

"How confoundedly nasty," I heard Gröning, who took care of the diving rudder, growl.

Now the entire ballast shifted. We had to make the boat heavier in the stern, had to shift the ballast of the heretofore well-balanced boat and pump ballast water out of the bow to pour water into the stern tanks, in order to make the bow lighter and the stern heavier. After a few litres of water had exchanged places the boat changed her mind and again placed herself in a horizontal position. Then she arose quickly and satisfactorily, but showed a tendency to list toward the stern, until we, by a new shift of the ballast, had re-established the old conditions of equilibrium.

After the boat had pulled loose with apparent reluctance from her bed on the bottom, she could not get up fast enough to stick her nose into the fresh air. Having the ballast diminished by nine hundred litres, she leaped upwards rapidly, but this did not suit my purpose, as I preferred first to put up the periscope and find out whether the atmosphere was free from British germs. As I felt I was entirely responsible for my boat's health, I entertained one fear, based on experience, that germs in the form of destroyers and trawlers, appearing suddenly, might endanger it. I made the boat obey my will, let the nine hundred litres be pumped into her again, and thus checked her quick ascent.

At the same time I had the dynamo motors started, so that we would have steerageway for the diving rudder, and commanded that the U-boat should stop at the depth of twenty metres. Thereafter, I soon came to the periscope depth and took a look around to see if I could discover any ships. There was nothing in sight, but woe—a heavy storm!

"Well, it can't be helped," I said softly to myself.

I made another careful search of the horizon and then arose entirely to the surface. What a delightful sensation to be standing on the tower with my hands to my sides and greedily sucking my lungs full of the fresh sea air! The air at the bottom had not been so bad. On the contrary, the engineers had kept it in first-class condition during the night, but more delightful was the wonderful ocean air.

Now the ventilator burst open and refreshed those inside with fresh air throughout the ship.

"Now, Mate," I ordered, "let me take a look at the map once more. That's right. Put it right up here on the tower—no harm done if it gets wet. Now let's have a compass and a lead pencil—thanks. Watch carefully and follow my calculations to see I make no mistake. From here to the first mine field it is twenty-two miles; from there to the second mine field about fourteen miles—which makes thirty-six miles altogether. We must reach the first field just before the ebb tide, as the mines are only visible just before or right after the ebb tide. We get the ebb about ten o'clock, and it is now half past six. We can, therefore, go along easily at half speed and will have enough time to recharge the batteries. Is that right?"

"Yes, that's right," replied the mate, and quickly folded up the map, which he had shown anxiety in guarding, time and time again, against the waves washing over the ship, "if we only don't have to dive again."

"I don't believe we will," I said with confidence. "Here near the mine fields I think there are few ships sailing. So far as that goes, we are really safer here. The scouting will be on the other side of the fields."

Exactly one hour before the ebb tide we reached those sections where the enemy, according to the reports from other U-boats, believed that they had effectively blocked the passage with a mine field that stretched for several miles. I say "believed," because the mines, as before stated, were showing above the surface during the ebb tide and one could easily steer through the lanes between them. The blocking of this important passage was therefore for the enemy an assuring but somewhat expensive illusion. It was not quite so easy as I had expected from the stories and reports of my fellow submarine commanders to slip between the mines.

"Well, sirs, here it goes!" I said to both officers, who, like me, had crawled into their thick oil-skins and had exchanged their caps, embroidered with gold oak leaves, for the practical southwester. "Now, we'll see who spots the first mine."

In a drizzle of foam and spray we were standing side by side and gazed at the sea several hundred metres ahead of us. The ocean had within the last few hours become still heavier and stormier, and the wind came from the southwest and consequently straight toward us so that there was danger of discovering the mines too late, as they would be concealed from our sight with every roll of the sea.

Suddenly we all three looked at one another and then quickly at the sea again. There they were! Heavens, what a bunch! In all directions as far as the eye could see were the devilish dark globes, washed with the breakers' snow-white foam. We were so overwhelmed by the sight of all these mines that we started to swear and kept it up for some time without any interruption.

"It's outrageous! It's unheard of! It's terrible! Such a mass! And such a people call themselves Christian seafarers—a bunch of murderers, that's what they are, who can put out such dirty traps!"

With reduced speed we went toward the "caviar sandwich," as Petersen called the dark spotted surface before us. Now it was "up to" us skilfully to steer the boat between the irregularly spread mines and see carefully to it that we did not get into a blind alley. If only our boat did not hit one of those devilish things! It would be the end of us! But surely if we kept calm, we should get through all right. Certainly we would. We had a war-helmsman who was a wonder in his line, boatswain's mate Lohmann. He could thank his skill as a helmsman for his long career in the navy. If he was up to some deviltry—which, it is said, rather often happened in former days—it was always mentioned as an extenuating circumstance—"but he's such an able helmsman."

Lohmann, when he put his mind to it, could certainly steer. He could hit a floating cork with the prow. He was standing with feet apart in the tower and grinning so that his mouth reached from ear to ear. He always grinned when he stood at the wheel. But now that he had become the most important person on board, he was radiating joy and pride to such an extent that his little square figure took on a superior pose of careless daring. With his right hand he spun the wheel playfully, just as if he were experimenting. He had shoved the other deep down into the large pocket of his seaman's trousers clear up to his elbow.

Then we were pounding into the mine field. Lohmann squinted together his small gray eyes to a couple of narrow slits, spat first in his right hand, and then in a long semi-circle towards the first mine which we were just passing on the port side. He, thereupon, hitched his slipping trousers, lit his nose-warmer—a pipe broken off close to the bowl—spat once more into his right hand, and began a series of artistic curvings and twistings to weave his way through the narrow lanes. And he was as calm and confident as if he had done nothing all his life except steer U-boats through mine fields. I could leave him in charge of it.

After ten minutes we had passed the mine field. We estimated we had sifted through about eight hundred mines.

At high speed we then steered toward the second batch of mines.

Then came a series of reverses which made this the most eventful day so far experienced by any U-boat crew in the war.

It was ten forty-two by the clock.

Beyond the second mine field an English destroyer was patrolling. We had to dive quickly and go through the mines under the water, a detested and very dangerous proceeding!

The destroyer had not seen us. The sea became more violent; the barometer fell rapidly; the heaven was filled with black rain clouds. The clearness of the atmosphere disappeared, and the ocean was restless and covered with white foam. The sea washed over the periscope again and again with white-combed, rushing mountains of water, so that for several long seconds I could see nothing. Suddenly we were in the midst of the mines. I could make out those that were close by, because the water had risen so that only the tops of the black balls, which here and there bobbed up for a second, could be seen.

To turn away from the mines at the right moment was almost impossible. We were running straight for a mine—the next second it was on top of us and passed only a few metres from the periscope. At the same time, on the other side, three mines clustered together in a group were floating past us. It was a hellish journey, and the destroyer was all the time waiting for us on the other side of the mine field, and compelled us to continue below the surface. He had no consideration for our difficulties.

Oh, how he would enjoy it if we suddenly went up in the air, surrounded by a cloud of smoke and fire! Good God! Now we are about to give him this joy. I had already shut my eyes and thought we were doomed—because one of the mines had just struck hard with a metallic clang against the periscope, a sound which I will never forget until I am in a better world! But the mine, which I saw just before the wave washed over the periscope, had been carried away behind us and had better sense than to blow us up; it only twisted on its axis and didn't do us any harm. Maybe it was old and damaged.

I could not stand it any longer. I felt like a man trying to commit suicide when he misses his aim.

"Quickly dive to twenty-five metres!" I called down to the "Centrale."

Rather dash blindly through this hell than always see your last minute right before your eyes, and still be unable to do anything. But if, while submerged, a cable should fasten itself around the U-boat? The chance of getting through was better down there, I figured.

"Start the phonograph," I commanded, "and put on something cheerful, if you please!"

In spite of the new, beautiful "Field Gray Uniforms," the song which soon resounded through the boat, I heard twice a hellish grinding and scraping above the conning tower—mine cables which we had fouled. At last, after many long minutes, we were through the mine field. We arose and I put up the periscope and looked around. God be praised! The atmosphere, or rather the water, was clearer. The destroyer was several hundred metres behind us, and we had come through the horrible place without a scratch.

Aha! There was the first buoy—the first placed on the narrow sand bar. Now it was careful steering for the ship. We took soundings and proceeded cautiously. If only the current had not been so strong! It constantly swung us out of our course. I had to steer against the current continually.

"Mate, how far are we now from land?"

The sailor quickly brought up the chart and measured the distance with a scale.

"Two and a half sea miles."

"Oh, the devil! And, as yet, we cannot see anything of it. The air has been thickening. That's all we need to make things worse for us!"

The cruiser on guard now came rushing past us on the port side. It was not far from us when I pulled down the periscope for a time.

Who can describe my fright when I put up the periscope again in a few minutes and could not see anything because of the fog that had settled down on the sea! A dark rainwall also moved along the surface. And this was just where it was absolutely necessary for me to see. I must see where the channel began to be very narrow! Only one narrow passage about two hundred metres wide, there was, within which we absolutely must proceed. Every turn away from this—either to the right or left—would immediately run us into the sandbank. And now there was no sign of the buoy which marked the channel. In addition to this we faced a current we had not counted on.

I searched and searched for the buoy. The sweat stood out on my forehead, and the excitement made me so warm that the sights on the periscope time and time again clouded up on account of the heat from my body. The mate must continually wipe the wet glass with a piece of chamois.

"Now we should be off the buoy, Mate, but I don't see it! Good God, what are we going to do! It will be fatal—it is impossible to navigate without picking it up. And besides, the destroyer which is lurking behind that confounded rainwall and which at any minute can come up alongside us!"

The buoy did not appear.

Then the weather began to clear up. The rain thinned and the fog lifted a little.

First we saw land. Thereafter we saw the destroyer at quite a distance on the port side, laying a course towards us, and then—then——

All good spirits have mercy on us!

The buoy—our buoy—was to the wrong side.

And we? Great God in Heaven—we were going on the wrong course! We were running right for the sandbank. We must already be right on top of them. Disastrously for us, it has cleared too late.

"Hard a-starboard! Reverse both engines full speed!" There was nothing more to do. Then came the disaster! A jar and a whirring—U-boat 202 had gone aground.

6

A Day of Terror

What we went through was horrible. The breakers dashed high over the sandbar. They hurled themselves on us to destroy our boat, played ball with us, lifted us high into the air and dropped us again on the bar with such fury that the whole boat shivered and trembled.

We had lost control of the boat completely. The roaring breakers made so much noise we could hear them through the thick metal wall. Every new, onrushing wave tossed us higher and higher on the reef. Exposure was our greatest danger. Already the top of the conning tower and the prow projected above the surface—but a moment more and the entire boat would be plainly visible. Then we would surely be lost. As a helpless wreck, we would become a target for the destroyer.

Pale and calm, every man stuck to his post and clung to the nearest support, so as not to fall at the rolling and jolting of the boat. With awe, I looked alternately at the manometer and the feverish sea which I could see all around me through the conning tower windows. Oh, if it had been only the sea we must fear! But through the scum and froth, more merciless than the wild, onrushing breakers, the black destroyer, smoking copiously, steamed straight toward us, like a bull with lowered horns.

"We had better keep below the water at any price, even if we are smashed to pieces against the sandbank and the boat breaks up, rather than to be blown to pieces by the shells of the English," was the thought that flashed through my brain.

"Fill the ballast tanks," I called down to the "*Centrale.*" "Fill all the tanks full, *Herr* Engineer. Do you hear? We must not under any circumstances rise any higher!"

"All ballast tanks filling!" it was reported from below.

Oh, how quiet it was below! Not a word was uttered. No anxious conjectures, no surmises, and no questions.

A deep, irresistible grief clutched my heart. My poor little boat! My poor crew! There every man unflinchingly and unhesitatingly did his duty, and devotedly put his faith in me. They were all heroes, so young and still so brave and able. And I, the commander, had brought them into the very mouth of death, and to me, the only one who could see our desperate situation, it seemed as if the scale of death slowly weighed against us, because the destroyer, with horrible certainty, was approaching. His sharp prow pointed directly towards us. Soon he would discover the projecting parts of our tower and prow, which the breakers treacherously washed over, and then we would be lost. Soon a hail of shells would sweep over us, and the greedy, foaming sea would roaringly hurl itself through the open holes in our sides.

The filling of the ballast tanks had the desired effect. The boat lay down heavily on the reef and spurred the wild waves to greater efforts, and, though we did not rise any farther, the jolting increased in violence because of its added weight. It was a wonder that the boat did not go to pieces like an egg shell, and we all looked at one another in surprise when, after a terrific jolt, nothing more occurred than the bursting of a few electric bulbs. "First-class material," I thought to myself.

The mate who, over my shoulder, was keeping watch on the destroyer through the window on the port side, suddenly said, in his hearty, Saxon dialect:

"Well, well! Where does he intend to look for us now, I wonder? At any rate, he doesn't think that we are stuck here among the breakers."

"Mate, you old optimist. Those words I'll never forget. Great God! If you are right! Then certainly——"

"He is already turning," the little chap cut me short, and jammed his nose against the window-glass, so as to be able to see better.

I grabbed him by the neck and pulled him away, as my blood rushed to my head.

"What? What is it you are saying? Is he turning—good God in heaven—yes, it's true—he really *is* turning, all the time turning—now his broadside swings round towards us, now his stern—he has turned—he is departing. He has not seen us, he has not seen us!"

I remember that once, when I was a little boy, I got a roe-deer as a present.

I loved it a great deal and we were inseparable. It had to sleep on a rug by my bed. One beautiful summer's day we were playing in the sun on a large lawn before the house when suddenly a large, unknown hound came rushing towards my little pet and blood-thirstily chased it around the lawn. The nasty dog was about to run it down when my pet, with a shrill shriek, appealed for help. I was standing paralyzed in terror and could not get a word through my lips, when unexpectedly the owner called the dog back with a whistle. Then I threw myself, with great exultation, down alongside my pet, pressed it to my heart, kissed its black snoot, and cried and laughed with joy.

Those were my feelings now, when, with my own eyes, I saw the impossible—that the destroyer, without suspecting our presence, had steered away from us. Was it possible that he did not see us, when, according to my estimation, he was only about eight hundred metres away? Could the mate be right, and the foolish destroyer have only searched the passage in accordance with his schedule? "But," I thought, with a shiver, "how easily would not perchance a glance in our direction have betrayed us?"

Radiant with joy, I told the crew in the "*Centrale*" what a happy turn the affairs had taken at the last moment. A burden must have fallen from the hearts of my splendid, brave boys.

I then revealed my plans to the engineer:

"We are going to lie here until the destroyer reaches the other end of his patrol, which is about three to four sea miles from here. Then, at once, quickly empty all the tanks so that the boat cuts loose from the reef. At top speed, we will make for deep water and then dive again to a safe position below the surface."

Again a light rain-cloud floated slowly towards us and favored our plans. Soon the destroyer could be seen only as a fading figure in the mist. Now we could risk to arise and get away from our other danger—the fiercely rolling breakers.

The valves were quickly opened. At once the boat came up. The terrific jolting ceased. The hand of the manometer moved upwards, and, after a few seconds, the boat's broad, dripping back broke through the surface.

There is the buoy! Now full speed ahead! We'll be soon there—now but a few hundred metres more and then the game is ours—a game on which life and death depended; a game which would have turned our hair white if we had not been so young, and if we had not, through horrible dangers, been united by true and faithful bonds.

As soon as we had placed ourselves on the right side of the longed-for buoy we again hurled ourselves deep down into the cool sea as happily as a fish which for a long time had been on dry land, and suddenly gets into its own element again.

The first and most dangerous part of our journey through the "Witch-Kettle" was over, although not without its horrible experiences. The narrow inlet was passed and also the several sea miles, wide and free from reefs and other navigation difficulties. Thus we merrily glided about in the deep and, in good spirits, hammered and listened and felt our splendid, hard-tried, heavily-tested boat all over back and forth, to see if it had pulled through without a leak from the pit of the rolling breakers; and we soon all forgot. As long as the nerves were at a continuous tension we had no time to think about past events. And though we had happily passed through and over mines and reefs, still the day was far from ended, and our main task was still before us.

This day continually brought us new and unexpected surprises, so that, at last, we had a gruesome feeling that everything had united itself for our destruction. First there were the trawlers; then the motor boats, which in pairs, with a steel net between them, searched through the channel where they suspected that U-boats were lurking. Every time we stuck up our periscope cautiously in order to look around a bit, it never failed that we had one of those searching parties right in front of us, so that we must submerge in a hurry to a greater depth in order not to be caught by the dangerous nets. And if for a short time there was an opportunity to scan the horizon undisturbed, then the atmosphere was thick, and we were unable to locate the shores, which we knew were close at hand, so that at last we hardly knew where we were, as the currents in these parts could not be estimated. Since the famous buoy we had not seen any mark which would in any degree assist us to locate ourselves.

We kept to our course up the centre of the channel and trusted that our lucky star would lead us straight. Every half hour we came up from the safety of the deep and tried to take our bearings and then submerged again, disappointed. The crew, of course, must remain at the diving stations uninterruptedly.

About two o'clock the cook came around with pea-soup and pork in small tin cups. He also stretched up his arms to us in the conning tower with a steaming plate in his hands. I put the plate on my knees and dipped out its contents, thinking "The wild beasts are fed." The moisture, which forms in large drops on the ceiling during long trips under the water, fell down on my head and into my plate and left small splotches of oil in the pea-soup as a sign they were real drops of U-boat sweat.

We again arose to the periscope level at four o'clock. At a distance of five hundred metres, a scouting fleet was moving about. At the same time on our starboard bow a French torpedo boat with four funnels was cruising around.

I had a desire to fire a shot at this enemy, but the fact that such a shot would send the whole lurking fleet at us restrained me.

I have to admit that it was hard to hold back from taking the chance, and it was with a heavy heart that I gave orders to dive again. But this, however, saved us. If we had traveled at the periscope level for only a few minutes more, I would not be sitting here today, smoking my cigar and writing down the story of our adventures.

We were submerging, and the manometer showed seventeen metres. Then, suddenly, it was as if someone had hit each one of us at the same minute with a hammer. We all were unconscious for a second and found ourselves on the floor or thrown prone in some corner with our heads, shoulders, and other parts of our bodies in great pain. The whole boat shook and trembled. Were we still alive or what had happened? Why was it so dark all around us? The electric lights had gone out.

"Look to the fuse!"

"It's gone!"

"Put in the reserve fuse!"

Suddenly we had our lights again. All this happened within a few seconds and more quickly than I can tell it.

What had happened? Was it true we were lost? Would the water rush into the ship and pull us to the bottom? It must be a mine—a violent mine detonation had shaken us close by the boat. And the U-202? What were the consequences of this to the U-boat?

The reports came from all quarters:

"The bow compartment is tight!"

"The stern compartments tight!"

"The engine room all safe!"

Then the boat unexpectedly began to list. The bow sunk, and the stern arose. The ship careened violently, although the diving rudder was set hard against this.

"*Herr* Captain," Gröning, who was in charge of the diving rudder, shouted, "something has happened. The boat does not obey the rudder. We must have gotten hooked into some trap—a line or maybe a net. It's hell. That's all that's needed. We are jammed into some net, and all around us the mines are lining it. It's enough to set you crazy."

"Listen," I called down. "We must go through it. Put the diving rudder down hard! Both engines full speed ahead! On no condition must we rise! We must stay down at all costs. All around above us are mines!"

The engines were going at top speed. The boat shot upwards and then bent down, ripped into the net, jerked, pulled and tore and tore until the steel net gave way from the force of the attack.

"Hurrah! We are through it! The boat obeys her diving rudder!" Gröning called out from below. "The U-202 goes on her way!"

"Down, keep her down all the time. Dive to a depth of fifty metres," I commanded. "This is a horrible place—a real hell!"

I bent forward and put my head into my hands. It was rocking as if being hit by a trip-hammer. My forehead ached as if pricked with needles and my ears buzzed so that I had to press my fingers into them.

"It's a horrible place," I repeated to myself. "And what luck we had, what a peculiar chance and wonderful escape that we got out at all!"

It took some time for my aching head to remember chronologically what had happened. Yes, it certainly was lucky that we, at the right moment, had submerged deep. We had been at a depth of about seventeen metres when our prow collided with the net, and the detonation followed. The more I thought of it, the plainer everything became to me.

As we had run against the net, it had stretched and that had set off the mine. The mines are set in the nets at the height at which the U-boats generally travel, which is the periscope level. If we had tried to attack the torpedo boat or, for any other reason, had remained for a few minutes more at the periscope level, we would have run into the net at a point where our enemies had hoped we would—namely, so that the mine would have exploded right under us. Now the mine, on the contrary, exploded above us, and its entire strength went in the direction where the natural resistance was smallest—which was upwards. Without causing us any greater damage than a fright and a few possible scars on the thin metal parts, which might have scratched the paint, we had escaped.

Undoubtedly the Frenchman was filled with exultation over our destruction when, waiting at his post by the net, he heard and saw the explosion, and probably reported by wireless to the entire world:

"Enemy U-boat caught and destroyed in a net by a mine explosion."

And little I begrudge him that joy if he, as a return favor in the future, will leave us alone, because we had gotten pretty nearly all we wanted, as it was.

The day's experiences were far from ended. First Engineer Krüger appeared on the stairway to the conning tower with a troubled look.

"*Herr* Captain," he reported, "we must have gotten something in the propeller. Our electric power is being consumed twice as fast as it should. I suppose that pieces of the metal net have entangled themselves in the blades. The labouring of the engines is terrific and the charge in the batteries is being rapidly reduced, and they are becoming exhausted."

Were we now going to have this difficulty, too! We had already consumed a large quantity of the current, because we had been compelled to dive at our highest speed and this uses up the batteries fast.

"How far can we go on it now, Herr Krüger?"

The engineer calculated in his notebook, shrugged his shoulders thoughtfully, and said:

"If we do not consume it any faster, it should last us for a couple of hours yet. It would be better, however, to decrease our speed a little."

I pondered this situation for a time. In about an hour the tide would turn and the current would be against us. We would not be able to make much speed then, but, on the other hand, it would be dark, and we would probably dare to rise to the surface. The enemy undoubtedly believed we had perished and would have decreased his vigilance.

"All right," replied the engineer. "We'll stop one motor. There is no danger we will run aground. It is too deep here for that."

Consequently, we stopped one motor, and continued ahead at a reduced speed. At exactly five o'clock we came up again to look around. Hard by in our wake was the French torpedo boat steaming at a distance of about two hundred metres.

"Well, what is it now?" I said to the mate, and bit nervously on my lower lip. "It looks as if that rascal was after us."

"It must be a coincidence," answered the unperturbed optimist.

We submerged once more, but came up again after another half hour.

The torpedo boat still came after us, steaming along in our wake at a distance of two hundred metres.

"If this is a coincidence, Mate, then it is a very, very peculiar one," I said to him.

When it was six o'clock we again took a look around. The Frenchman was still after us at the same distance.

"The devil! This is no coincidence! I'll be hanged if this is a coincidence. This is intentional. We are certainly pursued!"

There must be something the matter with us. The enemy must be able to follow us—there must be some sign that enables him to follow us even when submerged to a great depth. What could it be?

I was pondering this impossible problem. The only thing I could think of was that when the mine exploded, it had caused a leakage in one of our oil tanks and that the escaping oil left a plain trail that betrayed our presence. It was impossible at any rate on account of our slow speed under the water, against the current, that by a coincidence and without knowing about it, the Frenchman kept coming after us at the same precise distance. I had to find out about it. We submerged once more, changed our course, and proceeded at full speed. If the Frenchman had really been able to see anything of us, then he would also follow us now when we changed our course and were going four times as fast.

At half past six I looked astern through the periscope and again saw, just as at five, half past five, and six, the Frenchman who, at the same speed on a changed course, continued to follow us.

7

A Lively Chase

The fact that the French destroyer continually followed us at the same distance made me certain. There was no doubt about it. We had been discovered and were pursued. Soon the Frenchman would call for aid and would have all the bloodhounds of the sea on our scent and following us. By this time our storage batteries had begun to be exhausted, and the water was a hundred metres deep so that it was impossible for us to lie on the bottom.

"Nice prospects," I thought to myself. To the mate and crew in the "*Centrale*," I called loudly so that all could hear me:

"Well, now we have gotten rid of him at last. Didn't I say it was only a coincidence?"

I wanted to relieve the tension on the nerves of the men, because I knew how they had gone on for days at a high pitch of excitement.

In my plans, I had counted on the darkness, which must come soon. We would be very economical of the power, so that it would take us to the point which I had selected after carefully studying the chart. We kept to the same course for half an hour. Then, when the darkness must have settled down, I turned off at an angle of ninety degrees, and headed straight for the coast, where I knew the depth would permit us to rest on the bottom, to wait until the enemy had given up his manhunt. This would be towards morning, I thought, especially if the storm coming up from the southwest should increase in violence so that the searching of the water with nets would become very difficult.

The point that I had selected for our resting place was far from comfortable. And it was marked on the chart, not with the reassuring "Sd." which indicated a sand bottom, but with the dreaded "St." which meant the bottom was stony. But we had no choice. And when the devil is in a pinch, he will eat flies, although he is accustomed to better food. We did not rise again, since we knew it was dark over the sea, but continued at a considerable depth without incident and slowly approached our goal.

About midnight, according to my calculations, we would be able to touch the bottom. And the storage batteries had to last up to that time. Krüger figured and figured and came to the conclusion that they would hardly last long enough.

Until ten o'clock we had heard our friend's propellers over us several times. Thereafter all became quiet on the surface, and, relieved, I drew a deep breath. They had lost the scent. It became bearable again in the U-boat. I sat on the stairway leading to the "*Centrale*" and was eating sandwiches and drinking hot tea with the other officers and the rest of the crew. It was almost twelve o'clock and still we had not touched bottom. What would happen if the computation of our location was wrong? This could easily have occurred, because of the strong current and our slow speed.

Half-past twelve! Still no bottom! Engineer Krüger was nervously stamping his feet and turned out one electric light after another in order to save power. For the same reason, the electric heating apparatus had been cut off for a long time, and we were very cold.

At five minutes to one we felt a slight scraping. The motors were stopped and then we reversed them in order to decrease our speed. A slight jolt! We filled the ballast tanks and were lying on the bottom where we could wait for morning at our ease. Who thought that? He who imagined that we would have any rest was disappointed. We were lying on a rock, and the tide turned about two o'clock, and the southwest wind swept the sea fiercely.

At the beginning, it seemed as if we would be all right, down there on the "St." bottom, but we soon discovered differently—when the rolling began. There was no chance of gentle resting, as on the soft sand of the North Sea, but, instead, we banged and racked from one rock to another, so it was a wonder the boat could stand it at all.

Sometimes it sounded as if large stones were rolling on deck and, again, our boat would fall three or four metres deeper with a jolt, so that the manometer was never at rest, and we had to stand this continued rising and falling between twenty-two and thirty-eight metres.

At last, towards four o'clock, we gave it up. At some of the joints in the ship, there were small leakages, and none of us had any thought of sleeping. We, therefore, went up to the surface.

I opened the conning tower hatch and let the fresh air rush against me. I had a queer sensation. It seemed to me as if we had been buried in the deep for an eternity and had had a long, bad dream.

But we had no time to dream. The storm had not calmed, but continued in its fury, and it was not long before we in the tower were soaking wet. However, to our satisfaction, the water was much warmer than in the North Sea. We noticed that the last hours had brought us much closer to our object.

It was the Gulf Stream that was flowing by us and which, in this section, is really warm, running between two shores close together.

The night was coal black. At a great distance astern, two lighthouses flashed, one white and the other red. It was easy for us to know our position. No enemy was in sight, so he must have abandoned his search as useless. Can anyone understand with what relief we realized this fact? Confidently we began to look ahead to success now that, at last, the dangers of the mine fields, which had been greater than we had expected, were behind us.

The exhausted batteries were quickly recharged, in order to be ready for other emergencies, and then, with our Diesel engines running, we went out into the open ocean, away from the unfriendly shores, to get some fresh air and to rest our nerves.

When the day began to break, we were twenty sea miles out and had already recharged the batteries with so much power that, if necessary, we could proceed for several hours under water. In the dusk of the dawn, we had a new surprise.

Gröning, who, by chance, had looked toward the bow where the outlines of our boat were becoming visible, suddenly against all rules, grabbed my arm. With mouth open, eyes staring, and an arm outstretched, he pointed toward the bow.

"What is that?"

I ran up, bent forward, and followed with my eyes in the direction in which he was pointing.

"What is that?" I asked him.

I hurried toward the bow, so as to be able to see better. The boat's whole deck, from the conning tower to the prow, looked as if it had been divided into regular squares, between which dark, indistinguishable objects were moving in snakelike lines. Near me there was such a square. I stooped down and picked up a steel cord about as thick as my finger. A net, I thought, certainly a net.

"We have the remnants of the net all over us," I shouted through the noise of the storm to Gröning. "Get the nippers, hammer, and chisel ready. As soon as it is light enough, we must go to work to cut it free."

And the thick, dark snake—what was that? It came up to starboard, slipped across the deck, and disappeared to port into the darkness. It did not take us long to find out what kind of a snake it was, and I comprehended everything fully. That persistent, mysterious pursuit by the Frenchman was at once plain. Now I understood clearly what had happened on the surface after the explosion of the mine. My heart froze when I thought how readily the enemy had been able to follow our course.

We could easily trace the snake with all its curves, as it became lighter, because it was a long cork hawser, made for the purpose of sustaining the net. This was of light cork of about the thickness of a forearm and was light brown in colour.

About two hundred metres of this easily perceptible hawser were floating on the water, and gave us a tail with many curves in it. This tail, which we had been dragging after us, gave us the solution of the puzzling pursuit.

When we had torn the net, with our engines at their highest speed, a large piece of it to which the hawser was fastened had clung to our U-boat and, after we had submerged, the hawser was still floating on the surface and continued to drag along behind us, still floating when we had submerged to a great depth. The Frenchman, who had discovered us on account of the explosion, had observed this, and, in spite of all our twistings and turnings, could follow us easily.

It was a master work of our able sea crew to cut clear that heavy steel net. The sea became still higher and washed furiously over the deck, angered by the resistance of our little nutshell. The men were standing up to their stomachs in the white, foaming waves, and had to use all their strength to stand against their force. Full of anxiety, I sat in the conning tower with a life-saving buoy ready and followed closely with worried eyes every move of my men during their dangerous work.

All went well, and, after a half hour's hard work, we were rid of the troublesome net. The nippers, hammer, and chisel and six drenched sailors disappeared down the conning tower. Each of the six held in his numbed, wet fist a rusty piece of the net as a souvenir of the fourteenth day of April.

The sun arose as if nothing had happened. From the eastern horizon it shone over the French coast as if to say:

"I am neutral! I am neutral!"

When it got up higher in the heavens and sent its greeting to England, it shivered and hid behind a thick cloud.

What was the matter with it? What was it that destroyed the joy of the greeting of the young morning? What was it yonder that wounded its neutral heart?

A steamer approached. Thick, black clouds of smoke poured out along her wake and hung heavily over the sea. She had two high, thin mastheads, two funnels, slanting slightly toward the stern, and a light-coloured hull with a high bridge. "A funny ship," we decided and submerged.

When we saw her clearly through the periscope after a while, we found out the discouraging fact that she was a hospital ship. The snow-white colour, the wide green bands from the bow to the stern, and the large Red Cross on the hull and the mast tops easily identified her as such.

I was just about to turn away, as an attack upon a sacred Red Cross ship could not be thought of, when my eyes as if by magic became glued to something I could not make my brain believe, something unheard of. I called Gröning to the periscope, so that he could be sure I made no mistake. No, I was right, and, to my amazement, I saw an insolence which was new to this world. No wonder that the sun had hidden its face in order not to see this scorn and mockery of humanity. No neutral sun could shine on anything like that. Only the moon could stand such lights, although they must disgust even the moon, used to dark deeds.

The ship, which was safe under the holy flag of humanity and mercy, was loaded from bow to stern with artillery supplies, and amongst the guns and ammunition there was crowded an army of soldiers and horses. Under the protection of the colours of the flags, which they were so atrociously misusing, they were proceeding in the daylight on the way to the front.

"Such a crowd!" exclaimed Gröning, and stepped back from the periscope.

"And such a shame that we can't touch it," said I, furious, and stamped on the iron floor so that it resounded. "I would like to have gotten hold of it. Such nasty people, such hypocrites! But it can't be helped. The boat is too fast and too far away for us to head it off."

Of course, we tried and went after it at top speed for some time.

But the distance became greater instead of lessening, and, with our batteries exhausted, we had to abandon the chase. Then we turned, furious and swearing, and came to the surface again after a little time.

It was a very unpleasant feeling, after a short chase, to have to lie with exhausted batteries, and limp ahead like a lame horse. Consequently we did not attempt any new enterprise, but remained on the open water for several hours charging our storage batteries. Just as we were about through with this work, there came along an insolent trawler which started to chase us. None of us had any desire to submerge again, because the sun was shining so beautifully, and it became warmer with each minute we headed south.

As the propeller, now free from the nets with which we were fouled, could give us our best speed, we immediately began the race and hastened laughingly and in good spirits ahead. Our boat cut through the waves with such speed as it showed when it first came from its wharf. The foam made a silver-white mane for us. What did we care if we got wet? We went at top speed, and, smiling, looked at the smoking and puffing steamer behind us.

"He'll never catch us," I said to Krüger, who had come up to the conning tower to ask if we were going fast enough, or if he should try to get more speed out of our engines. "Just keep her turning at the same rate, *Herr* Engineer. That's sufficient. It looks now as if we were gaining," I told him.

Our pursuer seemed to realize he could not overtake us and tried to anger us in other ways. Suddenly a gun flashed and a cloud of brown smoke surrounded the small steamer for a second. Shortly after that a small shell splashed into the water about a thousand metres from us and a water spout not higher than a small tree arose from the sea.

We laughed aloud.

"Such a rotten marksman! He wants to irritate us with a shotgun. That's ridiculous."

"That's an insolence without an equal," argued Lieutenant Petersen angrily, who felt that he had been insulted in his capacity of the artillery officer aboard. "We should not submit to this outrage. May I answer him, *Herr* Captain?" he asked me with eyes flashing.

"Yes, you may try as far as I am concerned, Petersen, but only three shots. You can't hit him at this distance, anyway, and our shells are valuable."

Grinning with joy, Petersen hurried to the guns, levelled, aimed and fired, himself, while the water washed around him up to his waist.

"Too short to the right!" I shouted to him, after I observed the high water spout through my double marine glasses.

The next shot fell close to the steamer. It became too hot for our pursuer. He turned quickly and went back in the same direction from which he had come. But the hunting fever had gotten into our blood. We also turned and pursued the fleeing pursuer. Show us what you can do now, engines!

Shot after shot flashed, roaring from our cannon. The distance was almost too great for our range. We had to set the gun at the highest possible angle in order to have any chance of hitting him. The first shots all fell short, or to the side, but at the eighth we made a hit. A roaring hurrah greeted the dark-brown explosion which marked the arrival of the shell on the trawler.

In vain, the trawler sent one shot after another at us. They never came near us. On our side, however, one hit followed another, and we could see that the hostile ship was listing heavily to port, and we hoped to be able to give him his death blow, when the outlines of three of his colleagues were sighted behind and to the right and left of him, approaching at great speed. Our only chance was to turn again in order to avoid being surrounded, since too many dogs can kill the hare.

Early in the evening we submerged to keep ourselves at a safe depth. We were very tired, because we had had thirty-eight hours of work and realized, now that all the excitement was over, how the nerves began to relax. To begin with, the nerve strain showed itself by the fact we could hardly go to sleep, tired as we were. And when we did doze off at last, we had many disturbing dreams. I, myself, lay awake for hours and heard through the open doors, in the deadly quiet of the U-boat, how the men tossed about in their bunks during their sleep, talking and muttering. It was as if we were in a parrot's cage instead of a submarine. Also I lived over again during the night most of the events of the past hours. The only difference was, peculiarly enough, that I was never the fish, but always the fisherman above the surface who constantly tried to catch my own U-boat with a destroyer.

When I woke I could hardly untangle the real situation, because I saw the French Captain-Lieutenant's black-bearded face before me, when, with great joy in his small dark eyes, he said:

"*Diable, il faut attraper la canaille!*"

8

The British Bulldog

In the morning a clear, blue sky and a calm sea greeted us. The wind had abated during the night and had changed so that it came from the direction of land, and, therefore, could not disturb the sea to any great extent. In the best of spirits, well satisfied and refreshed by our breakfast, we were sitting on the conning tower, and enjoying the mild air of spring and puffing one cigarette after another. During the night we had reached the position where, for the present, we intended to make our attacks on the merchant transportation which was very flourishing in that region. We crossed the steamship lanes in all directions with guns loaded and with a sharp lookout so as not to lose any opportunity to damage the enemy's commerce.

Shortly before dinner the first merchant ship arose on the south horizon. It was a sailer, a large, full-rigged schooner, which, hard by the wind, headed towards the French coast. With majestic calm, lightly leaning to the wind, the splendid ship approached. The snow-white sails glittered in the sun in the far distance. The light, slender hull plowed sharply through the sea.

With a delighted "Hello," we hurled ourselves on our prey. Above our heads fluttered pennants and signal-flags which signified:

"Leave the ship immediately!"

Sharply and distinctly in the bright sun the command travelled from our boat to the large, heavily-loaded ship, and the colours of the German flag-of-war, which floated from the mast behind the tower, left no doubt of the grim sincerity of the command.

Did they not have a signal-book over there, or did they not want to understand us? Ah! A flag went up on the main-mast. The wind unfolded it and, proudly and distinctly, France's tricolour could be seen. The flag stopped at half-mast—a distress-signal! The flag on half-mast was the pursued sailer's call for help. They understood our command and were now looking for assistance before obeying us. Wait, my little friend, we'll soon get that out of you.

"Hoist the signals: 'Stop immediately or I'll shoot!'"

The signal flew up. Now, look here, Frenchy, this is no joke; soon the little, gray animal, which is circling around you, will bite.

"We will give, them three minutes to consider the matter, then we'll shoot down the masts," I said to Lieutenant Petersen, who was standing by the guns, and, in his excitement, was stepping from one foot to another.

With watch in hand, I counted three full minutes. The sailer did not take any notice of us, just as if our existence had nothing to do with him.

"Such impudence," I murmured, as I put down my watch. Soon thereafter resounded through the entire boat:

"Fire!"

"Rrrrrms!" the guns thundered with a deafening roar, and the shell whistled through the schooner's high rigging, in which it tore a large hole, struck the main-yard of the forward mast, exploded, and snapped off the heavy mast, so that, with its sails, it fell like a broken wing on the deck of the ship.

The results were immediately apparent. The red and white pennant, which in the international language means: "I understand!" flew to the masthead. The sailors, who had gathered in groups, looked at us in alarm. They were scattered by the commands of the captain and hurried in all directions to their posts. Giving orders in the singing accents of the French language, the sails were soon lowered and the ship slowed up. The boats were swung out and made ready, and men, with life-saving buoys, were running all over in great excitement.

We closed in on the ship to windward, and I called to the captain to make haste—that I would give him just ten minutes more to get away before torpedoing his ship.

In the bow compartment, where the torpedo tubes are built into the U-boat and the torpedoes themselves are stored, there was feverish activity from the minute we saw the hostile ship and the alarm was sounded. It is cramped in the forward part of a U-boat, very cramped, and it is necessary to have a special crew of very skilled men to be able to accomplish their purpose in this network of tubes, valves, and pumps. The officers' mess, which is just back of the torpedo compartment, is quite roomy and comfortable. It was now changed in a moment to an uninhabitable place. Ready hands pulled down the oil-stained curtains in front of the bunks and folded up the narrow table and the four chairs without backs. These were all placed in a corner hurriedly, and the luxuries were all gone, making room to handle the torpedoes.

Schweckerle, in command of the torpedo tubes, was like a father in the way he watched over his torpedoes. He loved them as if they were children and continually oiled and greased them and examined them carefully. They said of him that he mourned when he had to separate himself from one of them. And I, myself, saw that when a torpedo, for some reason or other slightly turned, did not strike its target, he went around broken-hearted for many days and could not eat.

This faithful fellow was now busily occupied taking care of his children and had selected *"Flink"* and *"Reissteufel"* (these were his names for the two torpedoes now ready for the tubes) when the command was given:

"First torpedo tube ready!"

This meant *"Reissteufel"* was to go.

Schweckerle was in his element and, when he gave his commands, the sailors ran as if the devil was at their heels.

"You here! You there! You take that! You take the other! Forward! Hurry! Take hold! Get the oil can! That's good! That's enough! Now put it in—push it forward! Now hold back! Slowly—slowly—stop!"

One last word of encouragement to the torpedo disappearing into the tube! At last the parting glance, and Schweckerle slammed the tube shut, and *"Reissteufel"* was ready to go on his way.

At once this was reported to me in the conning tower, but only a few of the allotted ten minutes had passed and we had plenty of time. We took a closer look at the sailing ship before we sent her to the bottom for good. She was a large modern ship, constructed entirely of steel, and had the latest equipment over all, even in the rigging. She could carry a cargo of from three to four thousand tons and, without doubt, had come from a long distance, because sailing ships of this size do not travel along the coast. What kind of a cargo did she carry?

The French crew stepped into her boats and left their ship. The last boat was capsized, when it was launched, and all in it fell into the sea. Another one of the boats came quickly to the rescue and picked up the swimming and struggling sailors. When all had been saved, I turned our prow toward the sailing ship, which was now lying absolutely still, and fired our first torpedo.

Poor Schweckerle! There it goes, but it heads straight, Schweckerle, true as an arrow. Bravo, Schweckerle! The French in the lifeboats, who had approached us where they believed themselves safest, yelled in terror when the detonation followed and the water spout was thrown high above the mastheads.

"*Oh, mon Dieu! Mon Dieu! Notre pauvre vaisseau!*"

"Poor devils," I thought. "I understand how you feel over your beautiful, fine ship, but why didn't you stay at home? Why do you go to sea when you know what threatens? Why do you or your governments force us to destroy your ships wherever we can find them? Do you think we are going to wait until our own women and children starve and let you keep your bread baskets full before we defend ourselves? You have started it. You are responsible for the consequences. If you would discontinue your inhuman way of carrying on the war, then we would let your sailing ships and steamers pass unmolested, when they do not carry contraband. You have wanted war to the knife. Good, we have accepted your challenge."

The sailing ship sank rapidly by the stern, turning over on her side until the yard arms touched the water and the red bottom could be seen. And, at last, when the pressure burst the forward cargo hatch, there was a shower of corn, and the proud ship, with a dying gurgle, disappeared into the deep.

The captain came aboard us. He never lost for a minute his personality as a polite Frenchman with elegant manners. He swung himself into the conning tower, smiled with the pleasantry of a *boulevardier*, and, with a gracious bow, handed his ship's papers to "*mon capitaine*." In the most polite and courteous German, I offered him a cigarette, for which he thanked me with a smile, as if we had been the best of friends for years. We questioned him. From where was he coming and where bound? He answered frankly and showed us without requesting it what a valuable catch we had made. It impressed him greatly how we were travelling about in our little shell, and there was no doubt he had an inclination to go along with us on our sea-robbing voyage, if he could have done it.

When I asked him why he had not obeyed our signals to stop, he acted as innocent as a new-born baby, and assured us that he never saw our signals. Indeed, he went so far as to say he had not even observed our U-boat until we fired our gun. When I pointed out to him that he had hoisted the signal of distress long before that and that this made his story hardly believable, he dropped the subject with great skill and gave the conversation a new turn. It was impossible to catch this smooth Frenchman, and when I had him cornered so that another man would not have known what to say, he slipped through the conversation like an eel with his great politeness.

I was struck with surprise to see his men so well dressed, washed, and shaved. I, a "barbarian," did not want to be behind the Frenchman in point of manners, so I complimented him on his crew's splendid appearance. Then he began to lament.

"Oh, my poor boys," he complained. "They have not looked so well throughout our voyage, but only today they have been scrubbing themselves, because they hoped to be able to get ashore tonight. See this, *mon capitaine*," he continued and opened his log—"on January 23rd we cleared from Saigon and have sailed nearly around the world, and now, only a few hours before reaching our port, we are met with such a disaster. What a tragedy! What a tragedy!"

I consoled him the best I could and promised to assist them so that they could land at the same time they had hoped. Then I, as he was about to leave the U-boat, offered him another cigarette, shook his hand amicably, and sent him off the ship.

We had agreed that I would tow his boats toward the coast until some new spoils hove into sight. Then they would have to do the best they could for themselves.

Soon after two o'clock, this occurred when the mastheads with the tips of white sails arose over the horizon.

We cast off from the boats, wished the Frenchman a safe journey, and turned toward our new prey, while Schweckerle made *"Flink"* ready.

As we came nearer, we discovered something that made us jump. We had been certain that the ship which was approaching was a large three-master, rigged somewhat like the one that we had just sunk, but what now astonished us and aroused our suspicion was that we distinctly saw, at times, dark clouds of smoke that seemed to be closely associated with the sailing ship which floated between and behind her sails.

"Anything that you cannot explain is always suspicious."

In accordance with this well tested rule for U-boats, we cautiously kept off a little, so as to let the mysterious ship pass us at some distance. We had heard too much of U-boat sinking to rush at anything blindly. What would happen if, behind the mask of the big sailing ship, a ready and fast torpedo boat was sneaking which, quick as lightning, would swoop down on us? First we must find out with what we had to deal.

We could soon make out what it was. At a distance of about two hundred metres in front of the sailer, there was a strong tug pulling the full-rigged ship with a thick hawser, so that it could make better time. There was nothing suspicious in this in these parts of the sea. It often happened that sailing ships were towed in over the final fifty miles of their voyage to reach port before evening, and thus gain an entire day. The large tugboats went far out to sea and tendered their high-priced services.

"Ah," we thought, "there is no danger here! But on the contrary, it looks like a grand chance to sink a ship, and, at the same time, send its crew ashore safely"—the thought we always had in mind when it did not interfere with our duty.

I rubbed my hands in satisfaction. We would give the crew of the sailing ship a chance to get aboard the tugboat and so send them home. Maybe they might also meet the shipwrecked crew of the French sailing ship and take them aboard.

At top speed we headed for the tugboat. First we circled round our prey to be sure that we would not be surprised by a masked gun and especially examined the tugboat, because he travelled back and forth daily through the danger zone, and would be more apt to be armed than would the sailing ship coming from a long voyage.

There was nothing suspicious to be seen—therefore we advanced. We approached the stern of the tugboat, slowed down, and, within calling distance, kept pace with him. Gröning, Petersen, Lohmann, and a sailor were with me in the conning tower. The tugboat flew the British flag. I shouted with the full power of my lungs:

"Take aboard the crew! Take aboard the crew!"

I waved with my left hand toward the sailing ship, in order to make my meaning clear. The commander of the "little bulldog," as Petersen called the tugboat, took his short clay pipe out of his mouth, spat far out from the bridge where he was standing in a careless attitude, but otherwise took no notice of us except that he may have thrown a shrewd, cunning glance our way. I thought he was hard of hearing and drew a little closer and yelled again:

"Take the crew off!"

The wind had increased during the last few hours and the sea began to run higher and was washing over our deck. It was impossible for us to use our guns—the crew would have been swept away without any chance of being saved—and we were, for that reason, unable to emphasize our commands in a desirable manner, but we knew what to do when the commander on the "bulldog" did not display any inclination to comply with our ten-times repeated order. I had a revolver handed to me from below and let a bullet whistle close to the head of the stubborn rascal. The Englishman seemed to understand this language better. He abandoned his careless slouch, blew the tug's siren, and yelled loud, sharp commands to the crew. Then he turned for the first time towards me, put his hand to his cap with a short salute, and next lifted his right hand vertically in the air, which, according to the international language of sailors, meant:

"I understand and will obey."

The crew on the "bulldog," which in reality bore the name *Ormea*, had, however, cast off the hawser and were now standing idly all around the deck with their hands in their pockets and looked at us curiously. The captain went to the engine telegraph and signalled "Half speed ahead."

"Ha," we thought, "now he'll turn and lay himself alongside the sailing ship."

What happened next took only a minute.

When the *Ormea* had gathered speed, it certainly turned—but not to port, which would have been the nearest way, but towards us. At the same time the skipper signaled to his engine room:

"Full speed ahead!"

The sturdily built, speedy tug rushed at us, pushing aside the waves with her prow.

We had, of course, been keenly observing every move made on the tugboat, but suspected nothing until that moment when he headed straight for us.

"The man is crazy!" I yelled. "He intends to ram us. Full speed with both engines. Hard a-starboard!"

But it looked as if we had grasped the situation too late. The tug had gotten a start on us in speed and came at us, smoking copiously, like a mad bulldog. The distance between us, which to begin with had been two hundred metres, decreased with great rapidity. Now the prow was hardly fifty metres from us. Our hair stood on end.

"Bring up pistols and guns," I called down.

These weapons, which were hanging always loaded, were quickly handed up to us, and we opened a quick fire on our onrushing enemy. Already I saw the captain's sly, water-blue eyes scornfully glittering and read the spiteful joy in his grinning face. He had good reason to feel happy. He would reach us, he must reach us, because he had greater speed than we had, and his position was more advantageous. Nearer and nearer came the moment when would stick his blunt, steel prow into our side, and the nearer he approached, the harder our hearts beat.

Twenty metres—fifteen metres! Was there no escape—no hope of rescue?

Yes! Gröning, the calm and thoughtful Gröning, became our saviour. He was on one knee by me on the conning tower platform and sent one shot after another at the oncoming target. Suddenly he caught the idea which saved us.

"The helmsman!" he yelled. "All men aim at the helmsman!"

In the pilot house with glass windows, stood the mate of the *Ormea* by his wheel with a sinister grin searching for the point where the blow would be most deadly. We saw him distinctly as he stood there.

Action followed immediately on Gröning's saving thought. We stopped the wild shooting against the dangerous prow, and all of us aimed at the helmsman and fired. Hardly had the first volley been discharged when we heard a shriek, and the Englishman threw his arms high and fell forward over his wheel. As he fell, he gripped the spoke of the wheel and spun it around. This saved us from our greatest danger. The prow which was to have crushed us was only about three metres distant when the tug was thrown hard aport, so that it hit only the air.

To show how close the tug was to us, as it swung, its stern struck our diving tank and left a scar as a remembrance. As the beast of prey after missing does not attempt another leap, so the tugboat put on full speed in an effort to escape. The whistling of our bullets and the loss of his mate had apparently made a coward out of a little tugboat captain, but we gave him credit for having been resourceful, after we had recovered from the excitement of the moment and recalled all the circumstances.

I quietly pressed Gröning's hand and smilingly touched the spot on his breast, there just below his brave, fearless heart, a spot which, in accordance with the command of His Majesty, the *Kaiser*, should be reserved for the reward due such a hero. Today that place is decorated with the black, silver framed Iron Cross.

9

Homeward Bound!

Why should I continue relating events which were coupled with less danger and were less remarkable than those we had already experienced and which I have already carefully described? The climax of the journey was reached at the encounter with the *Ormea*, and, after the climax is reached, one should be brief. For those interested, I can assure them that we did not let the schooner escape which had tried to save herself by flight, but hurried quickly after her, and, as soon as the crew had disembarked, torpedoed her. However, we regretted that the captain of the tug that tried to ram us escaped through her superior speed.

We were fortunate enough to make another catch on this same day, just as darkness was setting in, a steamer loaded with meat, inward bound from Sydney. We continued for several days through this fruitful field of operation in every direction and had both good and bad luck. Schweckerle had to bite into a bitter apple several times, as one after another of his children faithlessly abandoned him. But he had the joy of knowing that none of them went contrary to his good bringing-up and the care it had received.

Many successes we put down in our log and sometimes exciting episodes and narrow escapes, when our enemy's destroyers and patrol ships came across our path of daily toil, so that we should not be too presumptuous and careless.

Then at last came the day when we decided to start our homeward journey. The torpedoes and shells were exhausted. Of oil, fresh water, and provisions we had such a scanty supply left that it was necessary for us to return. It was impossible to tell what kind of weather we would have on our return trip, and, if it did not storm, there might be strong head winds to hold us back.

I decided to take a new route for our journey home. The Witch-Kettle with its horrors was still fresh in our minds and we preferred to take a roundabout way, rather than to run risks which could be easily avoided after a successfully completed task. In this period of thirteen days our nerves had been affected and there was little power of resistance left in them. It would not be advisable to put them to another severe test.

So it came to pass on the fifteenth day after the start of the voyage, that a great storm hit us and for several days kept us hard at work. We found ourselves far up in the North Atlantic where the warm spring for a long time still wears its winter's furs, and the sun never rises high. The icy, north wind, which blows three-quarters of the year, would in any event devour all his warmth.

Repentantly, we had again picked up our thick camel's wool garments which we had laid off in the southern waters. The further we went north, the heavier the clothes that we donned.

In addition to the cold there came a storm, the like of which I had never seen during my entire service on the sea, and to describing which I will devote a few lines, because a storm on a U-boat is altogether different from a storm at sea in any other vessel.

The barometer had been uncertain for two days. Its hasty rising and falling in accordance with the changes of the atmosphere made us suspect we would soon get rough weather. It was the night between April twenty-fourth and twenty-fifth. We travelled submerged to a considerable depth, and I was lying in my bunk asleep, partly undressed. At about two o'clock I was awakened and received the report:

"Lieutenant Petersen asks that the Captain-Lieutenant kindly come to the '*Centrale,*' as it is impossible for him to steer the boat any longer alone."

I threw on my jacket and hurried for the stern. On my way, on account of the heavy rolling of the boat, I realized what was the trouble. There must be a terrific storm above accompanied by a sea which only the Atlantic could stir up.

Lieutenant Petersen confirmed my opinion of the conditions which had developed during the night and added that he had never had so much trouble with the diving rudder before in his life. This meant a great deal, for Petersen was with me when our U-boat had been equipped for service for the first time, and had already gone through all kinds of weather. In spite of all the watchfulness that he and the well-trained crew used, the diving rudder's pressure was not powerful enough to resist the enormous strength of the waves. The boat was tossed up and down as if she had no rudder whatever. Only after we had submerged twice as deep as we had been were we able to steady the boat to any degree. We could still feel the force of the sea and knew the storm must be terrific.

When, at daybreak, we arose to the surface there was no chance to open the hatches. The opal green mountains of waves came rolling and foaming at us. They smothered the boat with the great masses of water, washed completely over the deck and even up over the tower. If anyone had dared to open the hatch and go out on the conning tower, he would certainly have been lost. I was standing at the periscope and observed the wrath of the elements. It seemed as if we were in a land of mountains which the U-boat had to climb, only to be suddenly hurled down again. I could see only so far as the next ridge, which always seemed to be even higher than the last, and if there had been any chance of seeing more, it would have been impossible in the flying foam and spray. The rain whipped the water violently and darkened the sky so that it was like dusk. The boat worked itself laboriously through the heavy sea. The joints cracked and trembled when the boat slid down from the peak of a wave to be buried in the deep trough.

We had to cling to some oil-soaked object in order not to be tossed about. Through the strain put on the body by the terrible rolling of the boat, by the damp, vaporous air, and by lack of sleep and food, we finally became exhausted, but at this time we had no desire to eat. The storm continued for three days and nights without abating. Then the sky cleared, the wind dropped, and the sea became calmer. At noon of the third day the sun broke through the clouds for the first time. Shortly before this, we had dared open the conning tower hatch and greeted the rays of the sun, although we had to pay for this pleasure with a cold bath.

We had been drifting about for three days without knowing our location. No wonder we greeted our guide with great joy, and quickly produced the sextant to find out where we were. Our calculations showed that, during the entire time, we had been circling around in one spot and had not gotten one mile nearer our port. But what did that matter? The storm was abating, the sea was calming down, and our splendid, faithful boat had stood the test once more, and, in spite of all storms, had survived.

We reached the North Sea the next afternoon and could change our course to the south with happy hearts. Every metre, every mile, every hour brought us nearer home. No one who has not, himself, experienced this home-coming can understand the joy that fills a U-boat sailor's heart when, after a successful voyage, he sees the coast of his fatherland; or when he turns the leaves of his log and, astonished, reads the scrawled lines which tell fairy tales of the dangers and joys and asks himself:

"Have you really gone through all that?"

Who can understand the joy of a commander's heart when, sitting by his narrow writing table, he is carefully working out his report to his superiors? "Have sunk X steamers—X sailing ships."

All around me were the happy faces of the crew. All were satisfied, every danger past and forgotten, thanks to the strength of youth and their stout hearts.

April 30—Nine-thirty a. m.

The lead was thrown. Now the water became shallow, for we are going into the bay—the German bay.

"It's twenty-four metres deep," reported Lohmann, who in his feverish desire to get ashore had been up on the conning tower since four o'clock, although he should really have been off watch at eight. He wanted to be the first one to sight land, because he is proud of his fine eyesight and was as happy as a child when he discovered something before his commander did.

"The lead shows twenty-four!"

"See if it agrees with the chart," I called to the mate who sat in the conning tower with the chart on his knee.

"It agrees exactly," the mate called back, after he had compared the measurement by the lead with the depth that was marked on the chart where we estimated we were.

"How far is it to land?"

"Eight and a half miles."

In five more minutes, the German islands of the North Sea arose before our eyes. Now we were unable to restrain ourselves further. We tore off our caps and waved them exultantly, greeting our home soil with a roaring hurrah. Our cheer penetrated into the boat, from stern to prow, and even set Schweckerle's heart on fire, where he was sitting alone and idle amongst the torpedo cradles.

Shortly thereafter we glided into the mouth of the river with the pennant bearing our name proudly fluttering from the masthead. This told all the ships that met us:

"Here comes U-boat 202!"

All knew by our announcement that we were returning from a long voyage and we were greeted with an enthusiastic and noisy reception. Officers and men thronged the decks, and in our inmost hearts we appreciated the great cheer:

"Three cheers for His Majesty's U-202! Hurrah! Hurrah! Hurrah!"

Thus the proud German high seas fleet received our little roughly-used boat.

At three o'clock on the afternoon of April 30 U-202 dropped her anchor in the U-boat harbour.

www.ingramcontent.com/pod-product-compliance
Lightning Source LLC
Chambersburg PA
CBHW032048080426
42733CB00006B/201